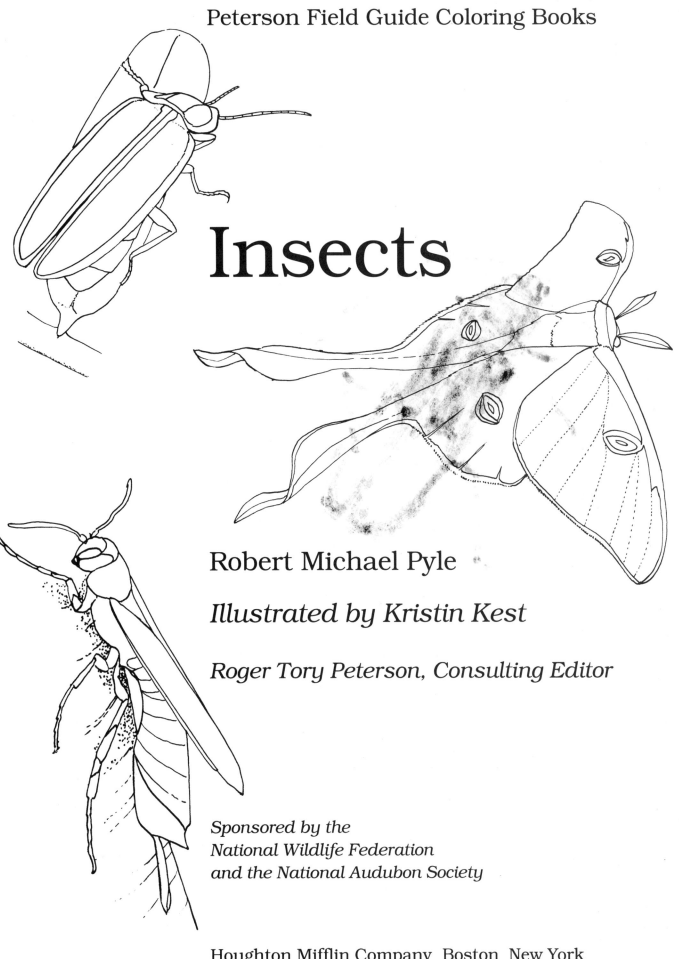

# Insects

Robert Michael Pyle

*Illustrated by Kristin Kest*

*Roger Tory Peterson, Consulting Editor*

*Sponsored by the
National Wildlife Federation
and the National Audubon Society*

Houghton Mifflin Company  Boston  New York

Introduction copyright © 1993
by Roger Tory Peterson
Text copyright © 1993
by Robert Michael Pyle
Illustrations copyright © 1993
by Kristin Kest

For information about permission
to reproduce selections from this
book, write to Permissions,
Houghton Mifflin Company,
215 Park Avenue South,
New York, NY 10003.

ISBN 0-395-67088-8

For information about this
and other Houghton Mifflin
trade and reference books and
multimedia products, visit
The Bookstore at Houghton Mifflin on
the World Wide Web at
http://www.hmco.com/trade/.

Printed in the United States of America

HES 10 9 8 7 6 5 4

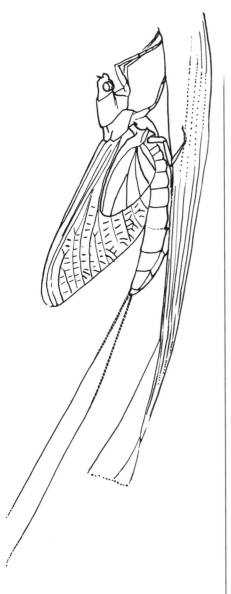

# Introduction

Observing insects requires a quick eye, trained to see minute details. Little things such as the pattern and number of wings, body shape, and length of antennae distinguish an insect from others like it. Most beginning naturalists soon learn to use Field Guides such as *A Field Guide to Birds* or *A Field Guide to Insects*. These handy, pocket-size books offer shortcuts to identification, with clear illustrations complete with arrows pointing to the special features of each animal. Many of the insects included in this coloring book, such as moths, butterflies, and beetles, are found in their own Field Guides.

This coloring book is for those who want to sharpen their powers of observation. By coloring the illustrations during evenings at home, you will condition your memory for the days you spend outdoors identifying insects. You will see the surprising range of colors in the insect world. You will read about the life stages insects go through to become the beautiful creatures they are.

Exploring the outdoors, watching insects and other animals, can be many things — an art, a science, a game, or a sport — but it always sharpens the senses, especially the eye. If you draw or paint, you transfer the images of your eye and mind onto paper. In the process, you become more aware of the natural world — the real world — and inevitably you become an environmentalist.

You will most likely find colored pencils are best for coloring this book, but if you are handy with brushes and paints, you may prefer to fill in the outlines with watercolors. Crayons may also be used. Don't labor too much over getting the colors just right; the purpose of this book is to have fun.

Roger Tory Peterson

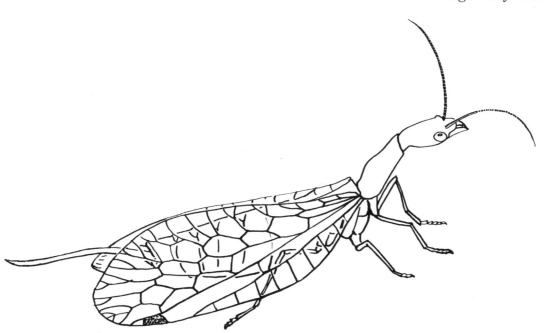

# About This Book

Insects make up the greatest part of life on Earth. They exist almost everywhere and affect everyone's life in both positive and negative ways. As the most successful group of animals on the planet, they have adopted a great many different life styles. This means that insect behavior and appearance are endlessly fascinating and almost infinitely variable. Given their vast array of colors and forms, insects catch the eye of the observant naturalist and make perfect subjects for coloring — from bright green praying mantises and katydids to purple, blue, and yellow butterflies, beetles, and bugs.

For many years, the Peterson Field Guides to butterflies, moths, beetles, and insects in general have provided curious people with resources for identifying and learning about insects. There is still no better place to look for answers to your insect questions. However, the enormous abundance and variety of insects sometimes seems overwhelming even in a selective field guide. This book will introduce you to the groups of insects and help you get to know some commonly encountered species in a painless and pleasant way. Naturalists of all ages should enjoy these pages. From here, you may find that the very wide world of entomology beckons further.

## How to Use This Book

Since there are so many insects, it may be hard to tell exactly which species of beetle or dragonfly you are loking at. But you can often get close enough for a really good look. By paying attention to the details given in this coloring book, you should soon be able to sort out the broad groups of insects you encounter afield. The insect names used in this book are species or group names. The name of the order to which the insect belongs is often given in parentheses.

### Parts of an Insect

Look at the simple drawing at the right. Virtually all insects have some things in common: three body parts (head, thorax, abdomen); six jointed legs; a tough outer covering called the exoskeleton; external mouthparts; and, in most groups, either two or four wings. Beyond these common features, almost any imaginable variation on the theme can be found.

The head carries compound eyes made up of numerous lenses; antennae; and mouthparts that might be modified for chewing, biting, sucking, or lapping liquids. The thorax bears legs, wings, and the muscles to power them. The segmented abdomen contains the equipment for digestion and reproduction. The wings range from the hard, shell-like covers of bee-

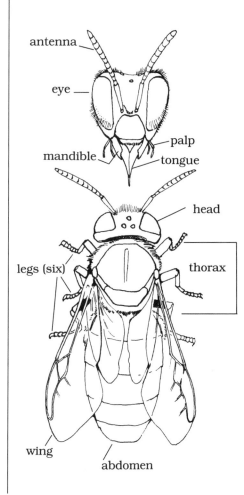

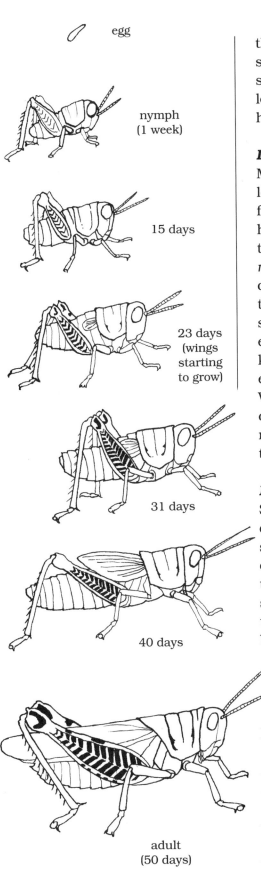

egg

nymph
(1 week)

15 days

23 days
(wings
starting
to grow)

31 days

40 days

adult
(50 days)

The lifecycle of the grasshopper is an
example of simple
metamorphosis.

tles to the clear membranes of bees, to the scale-covered wind sails of butterflies. You can easily tell insects apart from other small arthropods such as spiders and mites that have eight legs, from millipedes that have many, and from worms that have none.

### Life History and Metamorphosis

Many insects go through stages that resemble worms with legs. The fact is that all insects undergo dramatic changes from their younger selves into adults. In more primitive (less highly evolved) groups, such as dragonflies, grasshoppers, and true bugs, this process is called *incomplete*, or *simple, metamorphosis*. Their young (called nymphs, or if aquatic, naiads) change gradually, resembling the adult more and more each time they molt, or shed their skin. More advanced insects, such as flies, bees, beetles, and butterflies and moths, experience *complete*, or *profound, metamorphosis*. Their young, known as larvae, do not look at all like the adults but are essentially different kinds of animals, eating different things. When they are ready to change, they enter the pupa (the chrysalis or cocoon) and their tissues break down, then reassemble as the adult insect. This radical change is one of the most wondrous processes of nature.

### Finding and Watching Insects

Since they occur in nearly all habitats in the world except the deep oceans and ice caps, you should have good luck insect-spotting almost anywhere. Each species has particular preferences for hiding places and food, and these are what you want to find. Many beetles and others can be found beneath stones, loose bark, logs, and other moist dark places. Be sure to replace their homes after looking! Flowers host bees, flies, beetles, and of course butterflies. Collectors often sample the vegetation by gently sweeping their nets through the green foliage — every sweep is like a Christmas grab-bag, since you never know what you'll get! By reading the habitat preferences in this book and the Peterson Field Guides, you will get many more ideas of places to look.

*Always be careful with biters and stingers.* If you have an allergy to bee stings, never go insect hunting without your allergy kit. Most stinging insects will leave you alone if you leave them alone. A few, like some kinds of yellowjacket wasps, might attack if you get near their nest. But bumblebees and many other bees and wasps will let you watch closely if you don't touch them.

### Should You Make an Insect Collection?

On the whole, insects reproduce so abundantly that they can be collected without harming their numbers. Bug collectors are not nearly as good at catching them as spiders, bats, and birds. Making an insect collection is a most instructive

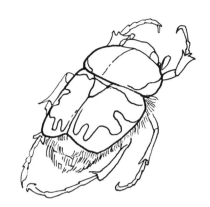

activity, and the number one pathway for young people to a serious interest in the life sciences. By sampling all the types of insects you can, you learn to recognize them sooner and you come to understand the differences betweeen the families and species of insects. It is fun to stalk and chase insects and to assemble a neat collection of your local types that you can share with other naturalists.

If you decide to try collecting, the Peterson Field Guides tell how to go about it. More and more people are freezing their specimens to kill them rather than using poisons, since it is humane and safe; besides, most insects freeze when winter comes. You'll need a net, and a box or jar to put your specimens in until you reach the freezer. You can use tweezers to place them in little envelopes to keep them from struggling and ruining their wings — this is especially important with butterflies and moths.

Then you'll need insect pins with which to pin and spread your captures for display. Most importantly, every specimen should have a label giving the date, the precise location where the insect was found, and your name as collector. Such details, called "data," make the creature into a scientific specimen rather than a mere curio. By compiling a list of your local neighborhood or county insects, backed up by a modest collection, you can make a real contribution to our understanding of the world around us. Never collect more specimens than you need.

Most people prefer to simply watch these small animals or to keep some of them alive indoors, watch their amazing life changes and behaviors, then release them. If you are one who enjoys live insects more than dead ones, you can get many of the benefits of collecting through close observation, photography, drawing, and keeping a field notebook and lists of what you see.

### Insect Diversity and Conservation

Of the two million or so species of life that have been cataloged on Earth, over two thirds of them are insects. However, recent studies in tropical rain forest canopies have led to predictions that there may be anywhere from 10 million to 30 million species of insects alone. Most biologists believe that the Class Insecta makes up anywhere from three quarters to nine tenths of life on Earth. Many thousands of species occur in any well-vegetated area.

Because they are so many and they are so various in what they do, insects are extremely important in the ecosystem. Yet some have become endangered species and many more go extinct yearly as we destroy rain forests. Because insects consume some of the same resources that we use, such as crops, timber, stored grains, and paper, and because some of them carry serious diseases, insects have long been thought of as pests. And since others are highly irritating or even dangerous with their bites and stings, or seem creepy, many people fear or hate all insects. Yet many more insect species carry out beneficial tasks, such as pollinating flowers, preying upon harmful insects, making honey and silk, and feeding people and other animals, than do harm. Therefore, instead of thinking "pest" when we think "insect," it is more useful to regard them as members of the same ecosystems we live in, some of whom compete with us while others help us, all while doing their own jobs in nature. We need to learn to work with insects more and to use fewer chemicals against them, since we poison our world in the process. In the act of wiping out competitors, we also eliminate beneficial insects and others we know nothing about. Gardens and lawns with little or no chemical spraying will have a better balance of predators and prey than a yard full of poisons. Clean landscapes are also better for you and make habitats that provide you with more interesting insects to watch and color.

The Monarch has a complete metamorphosis.

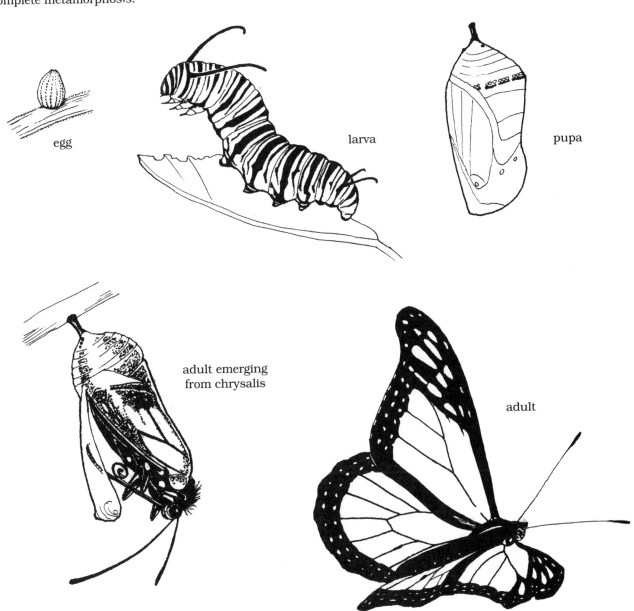

egg

larva

pupa

adult emerging from chrysalis

adult

7

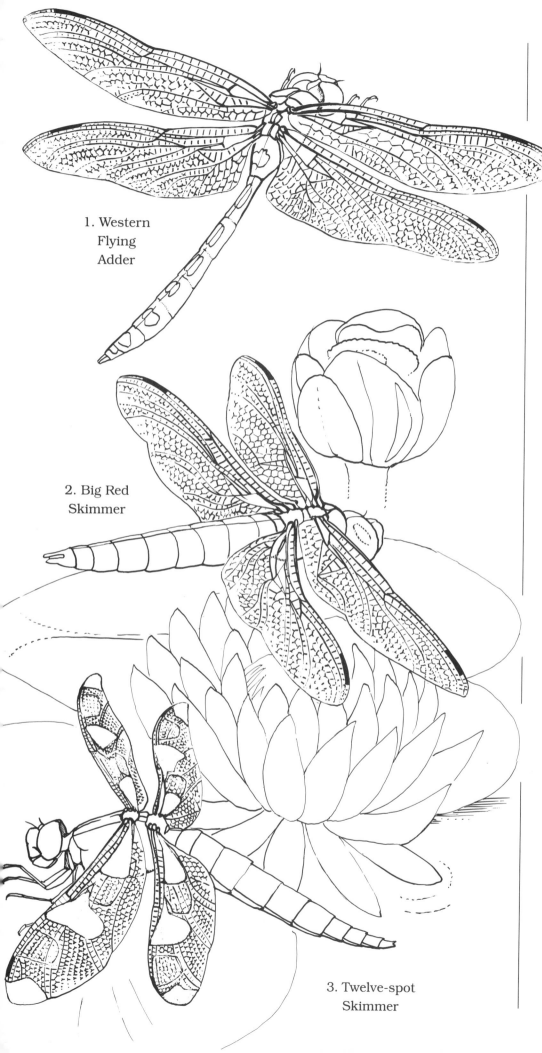

1. Western Flying Adder

2. Big Red Skimmer

3. Twelve-spot Skimmer

# Dragonflies and Damselflies (Odonata)

*You will often see these bright, active insects around ponds, streams, and ditches. Primitive relatives with two-foot wingspans lived near the time of the dinosaurs, but today's species span two to four inches. All four wings are similar in length, with dragonflies holding them out flat when at rest and most damselflies holding them up over their backs. The adults catch other flying insects, such as mosquitoes and butterflies, on the wing. Their young, known as nymphs or naiads, prey very effectively on small animals in the water.*

**Western Flying Adder,** or **Biddy (1)** The "adders," with their checked markings, reminded the person who named them of snakes, but "biddy" is another old name for dragonflies of this family. Look for this western type and its eastern relatives along wooded brooks and streams.

**Big Red Skimmer (2)** Like other dragonflies, this one has a dark mark near the wingtips, but you will notice it for its bright red colors and broad body and wings. It lives around stagnant ponds in the South and has similar relatives elsewhere.

**Twelve-spot Skimmer (3)** This bluish skimmer, and similar species such as the White-tail, are among the most dramatic of dragonflies. Watch for them around marshes and lily ponds, resting on plants as if to show off their bright colors, then dashing after their prey or chasing other insects off their well-defined territories.

**Green Darner (4)** Green Darners, and the related Blue Darners, are among the most familiar sights in summer wetlands all over North America. They are also among our biggest, fastest, and brightest dragonflies. Watch for their huge compound eyes, which shimmer in the sunshine and look like a space helmet. The naiads are fierce hunters important in watery habitats.

**Western Clubtail (5)** Clubtail dragonflies, as their name suggests, have thickened ends on their abdomens. They are also called devil's darning needles, but they do not sting or bite. You might see clubtails wandering far from water, shimmering and darting in the afternoon sunshine.

**Black-wing Damselfly (6)** The males of this beautiful species have blacker wings and shiny green bodies; females are browner. When you see a dark insect flitting like a butterfly along streambanks, flashing emerald green in a sunbeam, it might be this one. It occurs over much of the continent. Look for the naiads on the submerged parts of the plants where the adults rest.

**Civil Bluet (7)** Everyone knows the bright blue, black-marked damselflies known as bluets and violet-tails. This and related species occupy ponds, lake shores, and slow riversides all over the Northern Hemisphere. You often see two of them forming a flying hoop; they are a mating pair. All dragonflies and damselflies mate this way, with the male holding the female behind her head.

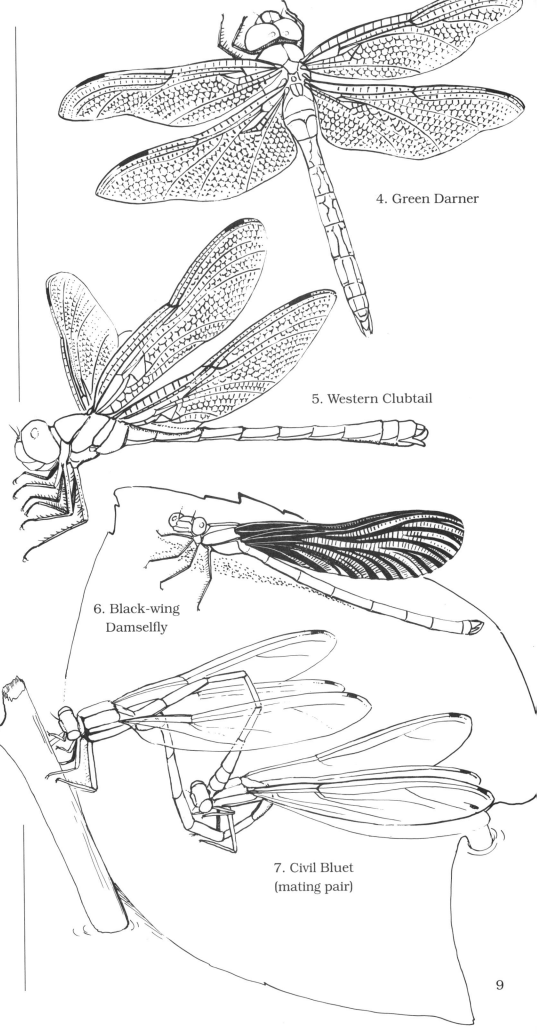

4. Green Darner

5. Western Clubtail

6. Black-wing Damselfly

7. Civil Bluet (mating pair)

9

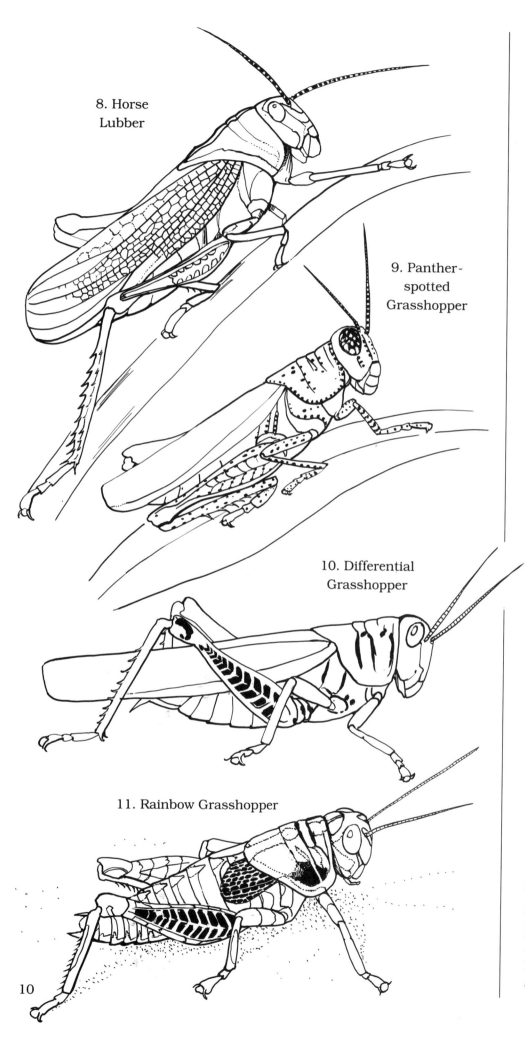

8. Horse Lubber

9. Panther-spotted Grasshopper

10. Differential Grasshopper

11. Rainbow Grasshopper

### Grasshoppers, Crickets, and Katydids (Orthoptera)

*Children have a lot of fun with grasshoppers, chasing them as they leap with their very long, jointed, and muscular hind legs. Many kinds can also fly, adding variety to the chase. When you do catch them, you often get "tobacco juice" on your hands — actually a bitter defensive chemical. Most are the same color as the foliage they feed on with their big mouthparts, but some are brightly colored. They make their songs by grinding scrapers on their wings or legs together, almost like the bow of a stringed instrument. Others, such as swarming locusts, vie with farmers for crops.*

**Horse Lubber (8)** This colorful grasshopper lives in desert scrub and oak woods in the Southwest. Like many others, it makes clicking noises when it flies, displaying its bright red wings.

**Panther-spotted Grasshopper (9)** Another bright grasshopper of the American Southwest, the Panther-spotted likes grasslands, where it feeds on the foliage of plants in the sunflower family. The female lays her egg masses, as do many grasshoppers, in the soil.

**Differential Grasshopper (10)** Common throughout the country in grassy places, this creature may be identified by the strong diagonal pattern on its hindlegs. It is a cousin to the abundant brown and green grasshoppers that enliven almost every yard or garden.

**Rainbow Grasshopper (11)** Spotting one of these brilliant hoppers is a real surprise. This and the closely related Painted Grasshopper live in the Rocky Mountain West, among grasses and alfalfa.

10

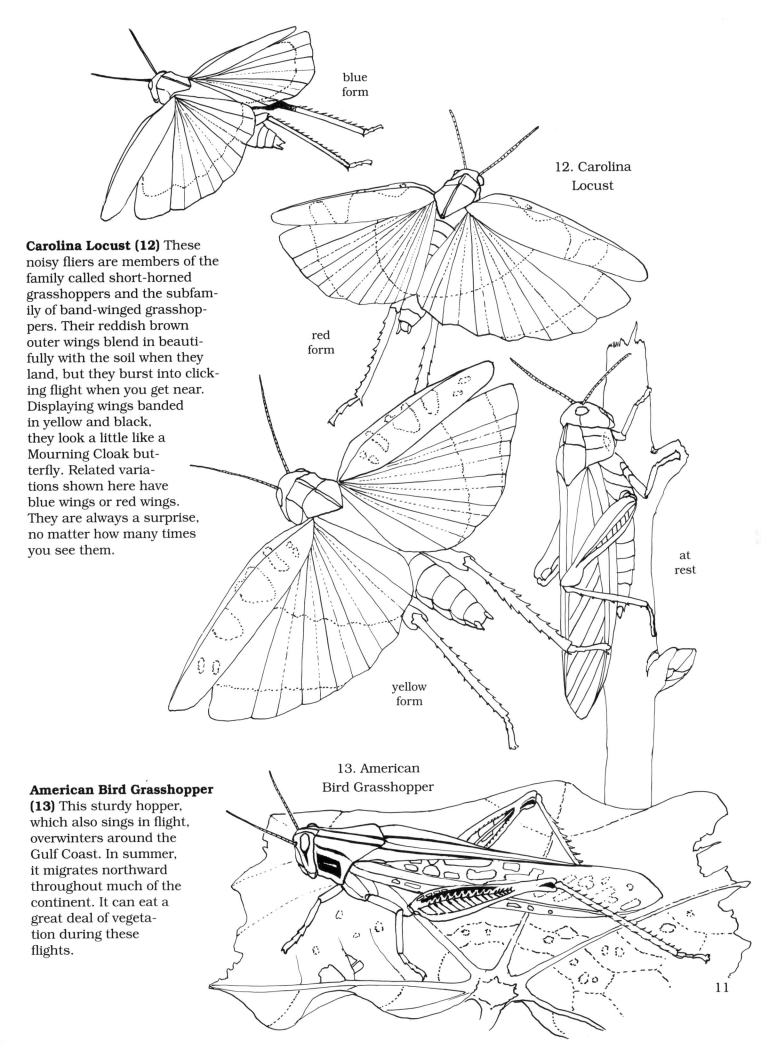

blue
form

12. Carolina
Locust

**Carolina Locust (12)** These noisy fliers are members of the family called short-horned grasshoppers and the subfamily of band-winged grasshoppers. Their reddish brown outer wings blend in beautifully with the soil when they land, but they burst into clicking flight when you get near. Displaying wings banded in yellow and black, they look a little like a Mourning Cloak butterfly. Related variations shown here have blue wings or red wings. They are always a surprise, no matter how many times you see them.

red
form

at
rest

yellow
form

13. American
Bird Grasshopper

**American Bird Grasshopper (13)** This sturdy hopper, which also sings in flight, overwinters around the Gulf Coast. In summer, it migrates northward throughout much of the continent. It can eat a great deal of vegetation during these flights.

11

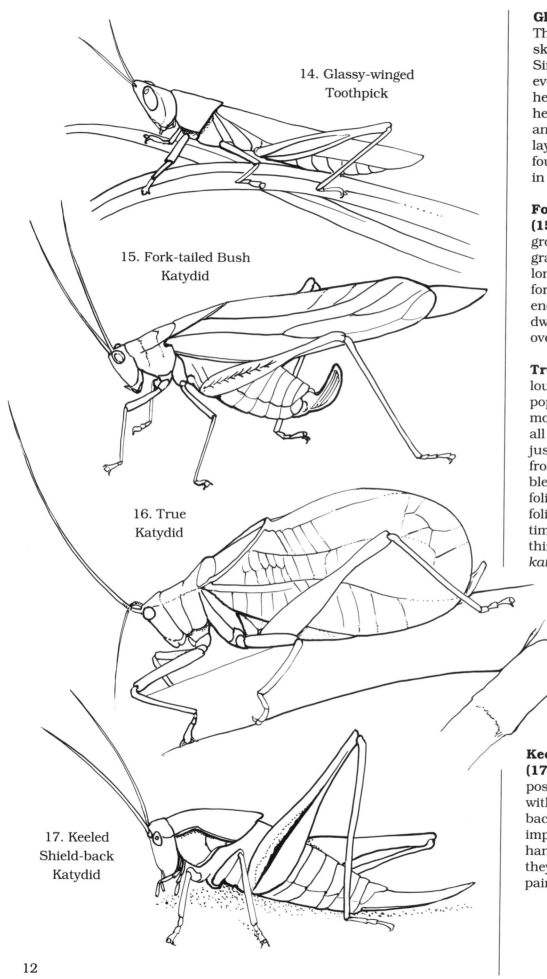

14. Glassy-winged Toothpick

15. Fork-tailed Bush Katydid

16. True Katydid

17. Keeled Shield-back Katydid

**Glassy-winged Toothpick (14)** Their name comes from their skinny, shiny appearance. Similar grasshoppers have even more pointed and slanted heads and are known as cone-heads, but they have long antennae and ovipositors (egg-layers). This wary insect is found in waterside vegetation in the Southeast.

**Fork-tailed Bush Katydid (15)** Katydids belong to a group called longhorned grasshoppers for their very long antennae. The male has a forked mating clasper on the end of his abdomen. These dwell in wooded landscapes over much of North America.

**True Katydid (16)** Its repeated loud song, *katy-DID*, gave this popular eastern insect its common name. You can hear them all over in late summer — but just try to find them! They sing from high up in their trees, blending perfectly into the foliage as they feed on the foliage of hardwoods. Sometimes their call stretches into a third syllable, and they say *katy-DIDN'T*.

**Keeled Shield-back Katydid (17)** This West Coast animal possesses a shieldlike thorax with a keel or rib down its back, and the female has an impressive ovipositor. Don't handle these grasshoppers, as they are capable of giving a painful bite.

**Jerusalem Cricket (18)** A very odd-looking insect, the Jerusalem Cricket has powerful legs and a head like a huge ant's. It moves slowly and often hides beneath rocks in its western haunts.

**Snowy Tree Cricket (19)** Its transparent wings make this insect especially difficult to spot in its wooded habitat, and its trilling song is equally challenging to place. The nymphs eat plants, but the adults are carnivorous. They eat aphids, caterpillars, and other small invertebrates.

**Field Cricket (20)** The cricket sings its chirping song for the benefit of its mate, but the sound has endeared these dark, scurrying insects to people for centuries. In China they are kept as pets in bamboo cages, and a "cricket on the hearth" was good luck in English folklore. Field Crickets often come indoors for the winter, bringing their friendly songs to our houses.

**Mole Cricket (21)** Like their namesake mammal, the mole, these robust insects burrow in the earth with their broad digging "forepaws." They can fly remarkably well when they unfold their seemingly small wings. The sound they make is more like a growl than a song.

**Mormon Cricket (22)** These heavy, shiny-dark insects sometimes travel across Utah roads by the many thousands. They attacked the crops of Mormon settlers in the mid-1800s, but flocks of California gulls saved the day and the crops for the farmers. The crickets could offer a substantial source of food in themselves, if we were willing to eat insects as many native peoples do.

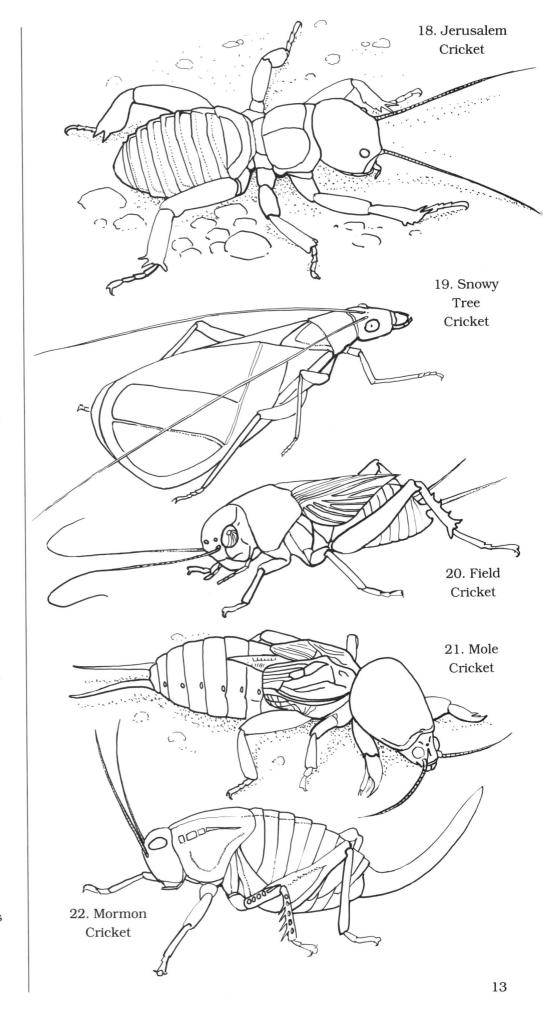

18. Jerusalem Cricket

19. Snowy Tree Cricket

20. Field Cricket

21. Mole Cricket

22. Mormon Cricket

13

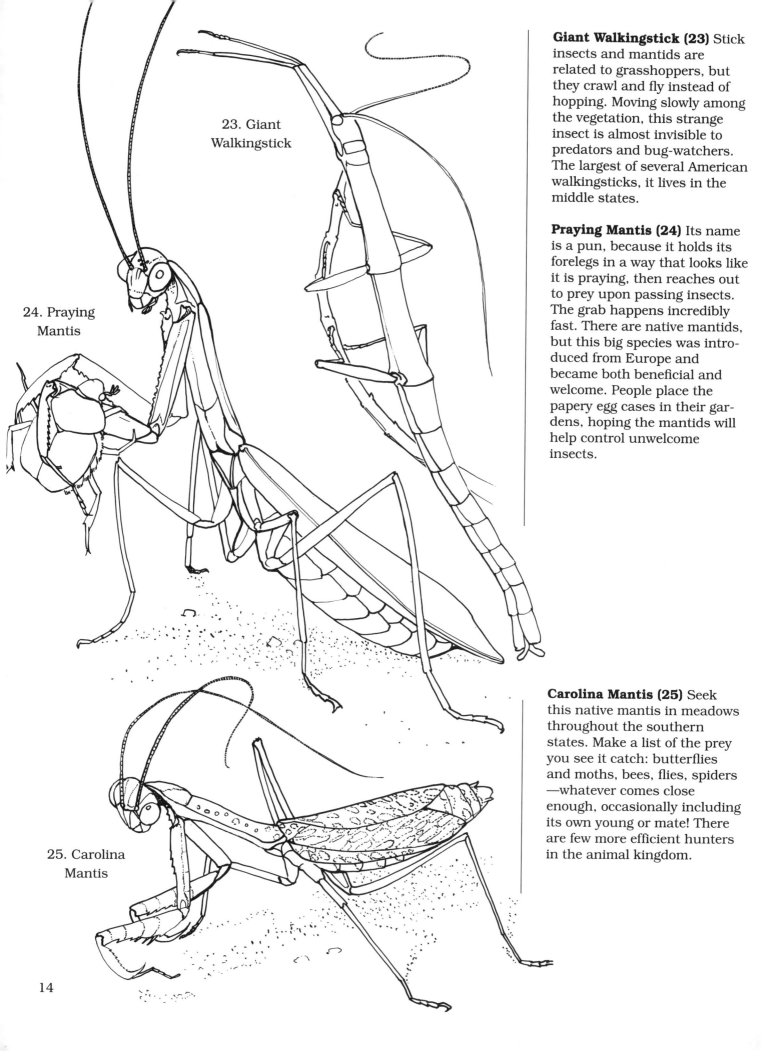

23. Giant Walkingstick

24. Praying Mantis

25. Carolina Mantis

**Giant Walkingstick (23)** Stick insects and mantids are related to grasshoppers, but they crawl and fly instead of hopping. Moving slowly among the vegetation, this strange insect is almost invisible to predators and bug-watchers. The largest of several American walkingsticks, it lives in the middle states.

**Praying Mantis (24)** Its name is a pun, because it holds its forelegs in a way that looks like it is praying, then reaches out to prey upon passing insects. The grab happens incredibly fast. There are native mantids, but this big species was introduced from Europe and became both beneficial and welcome. People place the papery egg cases in their gardens, hoping the mantids will help control unwelcome insects.

**Carolina Mantis (25)** Seek this native mantis in meadows throughout the southern states. Make a list of the prey you see it catch: butterflies and moths, bees, flies, spiders —whatever comes close enough, occasionally including its own young or mate! There are few more efficient hunters in the animal kingdom.

14

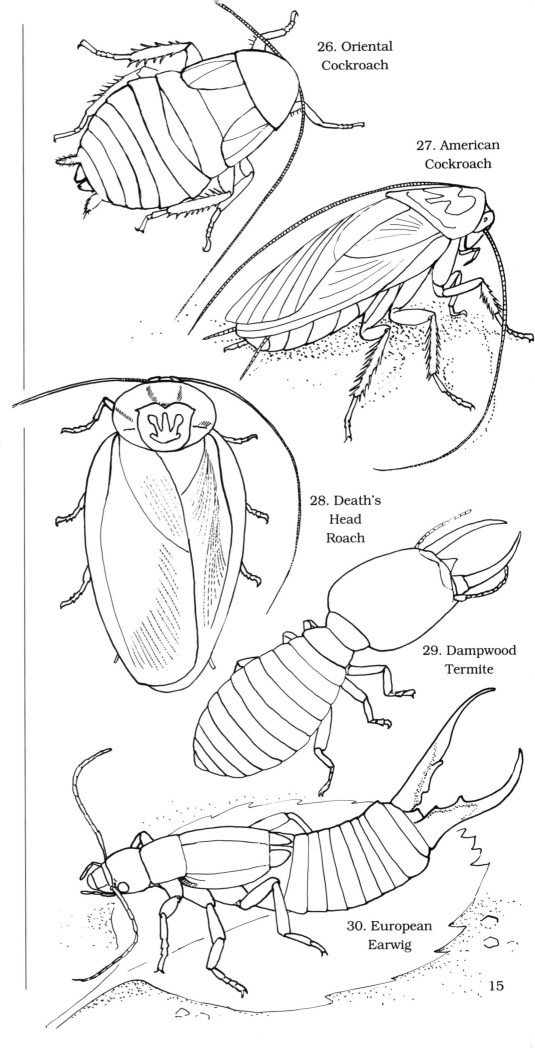

## Roaches (Blattodea), Termites (Isoptera), and Earwigs (Dermaptera)

*Many of the shiny brown insects that people commonly call "bugs" belong to one or another of these groups.*

**Oriental Cockroach (26)** This large Asian roach has been accidentally introduced into hot and indoor habitats around the world. Because it likes garbage, people associate it it with filth and disease, but roaches are actually quite clean in their habits.

**American Cockroach (27)** The sleek, speedy appearance of this roach, and its preference for dumps as well as kitchens, cause it to be hated by most people. However, it has been highly valuable in medical research and teaching.

**Death's Head Roach (28)** The markings on this insect's thorax remind some of a skull, leading to superstitions of bad luck and death in the American tropics, where it lives in forest litter. Roaches have existed in much the same form for at least 300 million years, making them among the most successful creatures on Earth.

**Dampwood Termite (29)** Termites have protozoa (single-celled animals) in their gut that enable them to digest wood. This species lives within damp wood, except when the adults grow wings and disperse to form a new colony. See the related **Subterranean Termite** on page 16.

**European Earwig (30)** These and native earwigs do some garden damage, but they also help control "pest" insects and do not crawl into people's ears as folklore suggests. Their pincers are for defense. A very large species lives in West Coast seaside flotsam.

26. Oriental Cockroach

27. American Cockroach

28. Death's Head Roach

29. Dampwood Termite

30. European Earwig

15

# In the Soil

The soil is full of various insects that give it fertility by recycling vegetation and dead animals. Clockwise: the **Leafcutting Ant (31)** farms a fungus on composted leaves that it has harvested. The **Subterranean Termite worker (32)** makes soil from wood. This **Globular Springtail (33)** is one of thousands of species and billions of individuals of these tiny, trigger-tailed insects throughout the world's soil. **Hister Beetles (34)** feed on fly maggots in carrion and other soil insects. **Silverfish (35),** or bristletails, glean decaying plants and are considered to be very primitive. The **Spider Beetle (36)** may be more advanced, but like some silverfish, it scavenges many kinds of organic material in human buildings. Other types inhabit animal nests such as mouse holes in the soil.

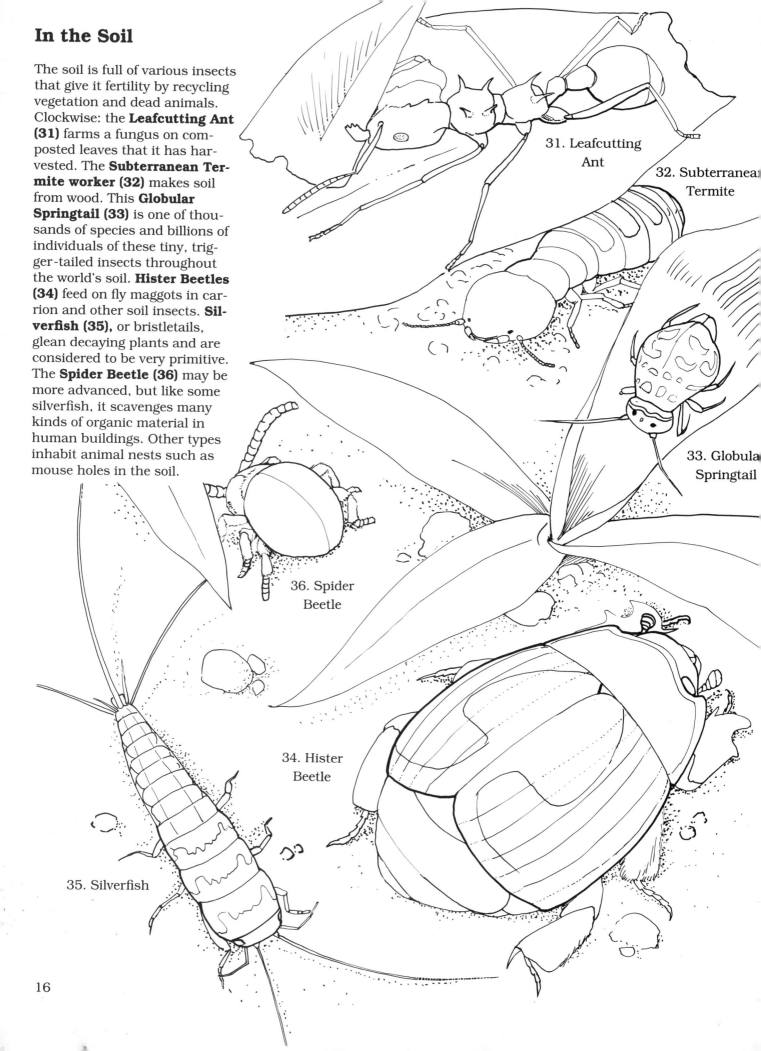

31. Leafcutting Ant

32. Subterranean Termite

33. Globular Springtail

36. Spider Beetle

34. Hister Beetle

35. Silverfish

16

# True Bugs (Heteroptera)

The name "bug" really belongs only to this order of insects. Their wings, part colored and part transparent, make a triangular patch where they fold over their backs. Bugs have sharp beaks used to suck plant or animal juices, and they live in almost all habitats, including the open seas. Unlike beetles, bugs have a simple metamorphosis.

**Cotton Stainer (37)** This bright bug lives in cotton fields in the South, where it damages the plants and stains the fibers. Sometimes it lives on hibiscus or citrus instead.

**Leaf-footed Bug (38)** Common in the East on trees, bushes, and weeds but hard to spot with their leaflike hindlegs providing camouflage. Kids like the related Squash Bug because it eats the squash, and for the nasty smell it gives off when squashed.

**Shield-back Bug (39)** The anchorlike pattern on its back gives this bug its scientific name, *anchorago*. It uses its formidable beak to prey upon beetle grubs and caterpillars.

**Harlequin Bug (40)** A harlequin is a brightly dressed joker or clown. This red, orange, black, and white insect is also called Calico Bug, Fire Bug, and Cabbage Bug since it likes to feed on cabbages, sprouts, and broccoli. The eggs look like little barrels lined up on leaves.

**Green Stink Bug (41)** Observant children know this bright green insect, also called Soldier or Shield Bug. The name comes from the odor it makes when threatened by predators or by gardeners unhappy about the damage it does to fruits and vegetables.

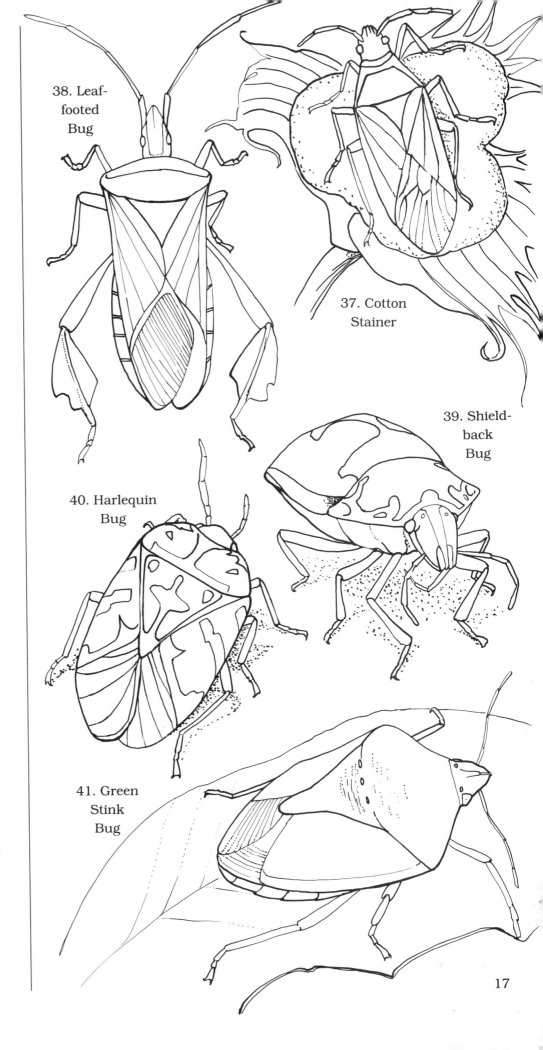

38. Leaf-footed Bug

37. Cotton Stainer

39. Shield-back Bug

40. Harlequin Bug

41. Green Stink Bug

17

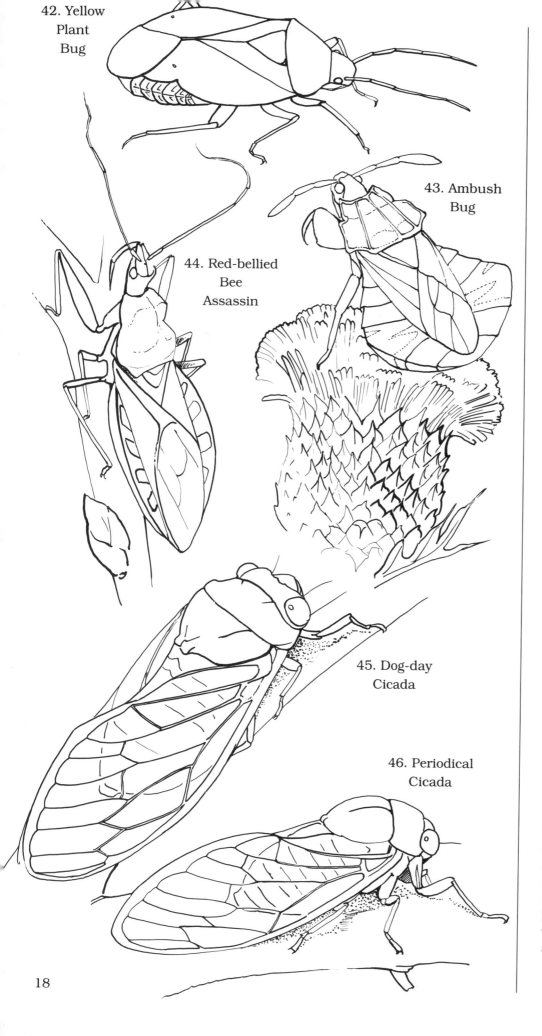

42. Yellow
Plant
Bug

43. Ambush
Bug

44. Red-bellied
Bee
Assassin

45. Dog-day
Cicada

46. Periodical
Cicada

**Yellow Plant Bug (42)** A resident of the East, this brightly colored bug comes in many colors, depending on where you find it. Watch for it feeding on wildflowers in shady glens and meadows.

**Ambush Bug (43)** Their yellow and black patchy colors and jagged shape make ambush bugs nearly invisible on the flower heads where they hide out. Once you recognize their looks, you can pick them out on many sunflowers and goldenrods. Then you can watch them as they nab visiting bees and butterflies with sudden strikes of their mantislike forelegs.

**Red-bellied Bee Assassin (44)** Assassin bugs, like ambush bugs, move with great speed to catch other insects in their powerful claws. This type specializes in bees — first paralyzing them with a poison, then sucking out their vital juices.

**Dog-day Cicada (45)** The big nymphs live underground, sucking on pine roots, but the adults don't seem to eat. They come out in the hot "dog days" of August after a three-year development, then mate. The males make a song that sounds like a saw cutting the pines they feed on.

**Periodical Cicada (46)** These are among our most amazing insects. One kind takes 13 years for the underground nymph to become an adult; another takes 17 years. When the adults emerge, they are so numerous that predators can't begin to eat them all, and the whining song they make is deafening. Each year's hatching brood occurs only in certain places. Changes in the landscape can wipe out the whole year's population in an area.

**Oak Treehopper (47)** You have a chance of finding this handsome insect wherever oaks grow. Its big horn looks like a leaf bud, but the brilliant red eyes stand out. The young first cluster together, then spread out as they grow and come to resemble the adults more and more.

**Buffalo Treehopper (48)** Its big hump and the horns on its thorax look a little like those of a bison, or buffalo. Of the many plants it uses, from cherry trees to cherry tomatoes, it seems to prefer alfalfa. More common today than the mammal it was named for.

**Sponged Treehopper (49)** These tiny treehoppers live in the Southwest and the American tropics. Their bizarre humps and horns have a spongy texture. Their odd form has a practical use in mating.

**Sharpshooter (50)** This beautiful bug lives in undeveloped open spaces in Florida, so it is becoming uncommon. Its habit of suddenly leaping at great speed and its bright colors reminded the namer of a blazing bullet shot by a sharpshooter.

**Red-banded Leafhopper (51)** This pretty bug is common over much of the continent. The numerous little green leafhoppers you see may be the nymphs of this species. Leafhoppers lay their eggs beneath the surface of plants. When they hatch and feed on stems, their saliva makes the leaves wither and drop.

**Willow Aphid (52)** Huge numbers of aphids suck the juices of the world's plants, sometimes killing them. Ants keep herds of aphids for the honeydew they give off. During the summer, females bear female young without males; later they reproduce normally.

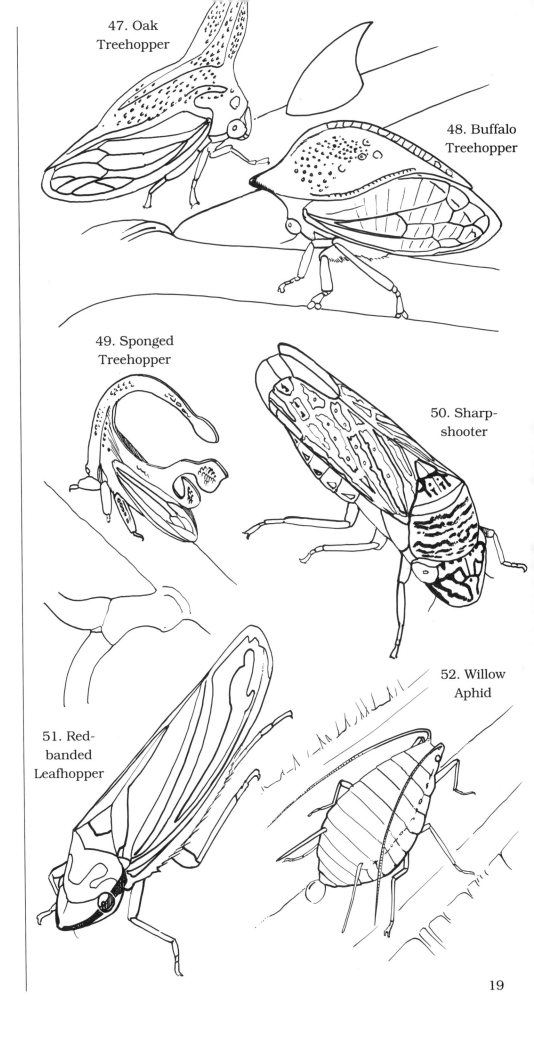

47. Oak Treehopper

48. Buffalo Treehopper

49. Sponged Treehopper

50. Sharpshooter

51. Red-banded Leafhopper

52. Willow Aphid

19

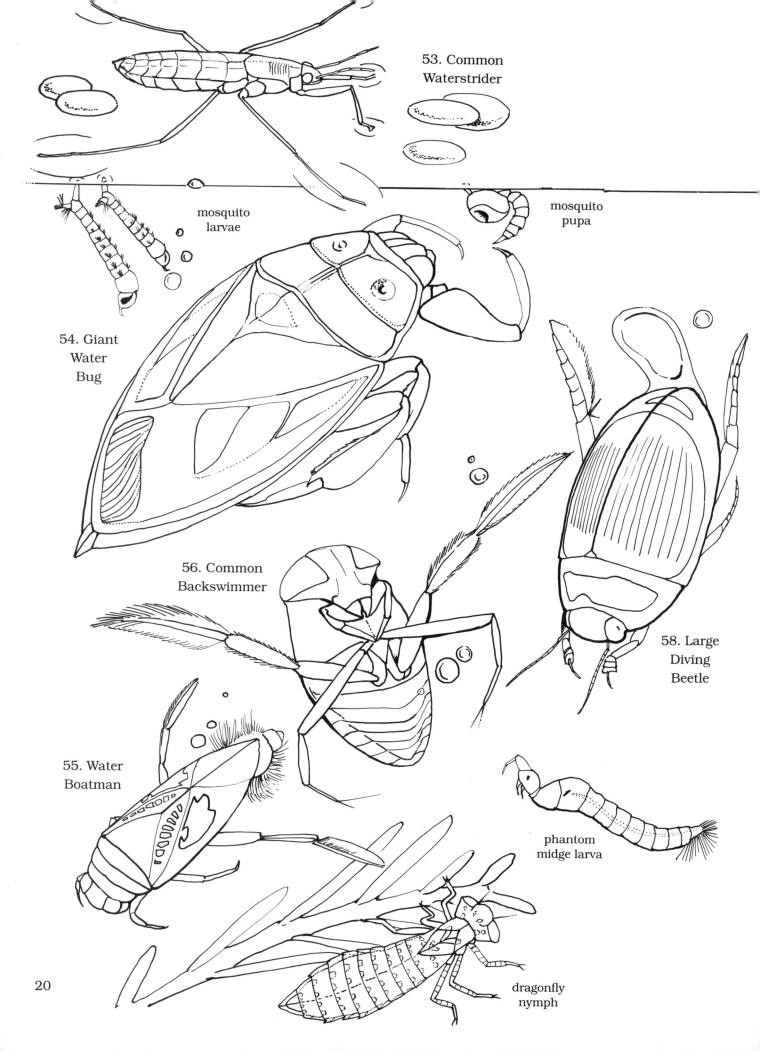

53. Common
Waterstrider

mosquito
larvae

mosquito
pupa

54. Giant
Water
Bug

56. Common
Backswimmer

58. Large
Diving
Beetle

55. Water
Boatman

phantom
midge larva

dragonfly
nymph

20

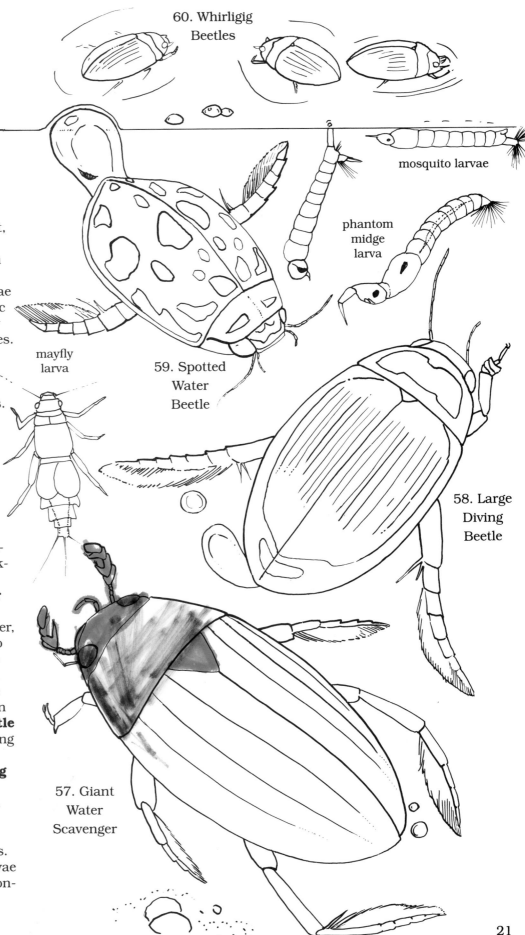

60. Whirligig
Beetles

mosquito larvae

phantom
midge
larva

mayfly
larva

59. Spotted
Water
Beetle

58. Large
Diving
Beetle

57. Giant
Water
Scavenger

## In the Pond

Counterclockwise from top left, this scene shows an array of aquatic bugs and beetles such as you might see in an unpolluted pond, including the larvae and nymphs of various aquatic insects. These are typical prey of the hunting bugs and beetles. Everyone knows **Common Waterstriders (53),** which waterski on bubbles and are also called skippers or skaters. The **Giant Water Bug (54)** is the fiercest water insect, snatching salamanders and fish and occasionally stabbing waders' toes. The **Water Boatman (55)** and the **Common Backswimmer (56)** both have flat, furry hindlegs that operate as oars, but boatmen graze on algae while backswimmers suck the fluids of animal prey. The **Giant Water Scavenger (57)** cleans up decaying carcasses in the water, often leaving the pond to fly to bright lights at night. A **Large Diving Beetle (58)** dives with its own air supply in a bubble pulled behind it like an oxygen tank; the **Spotted Water Beetle (59)** does the same, also feeding on small fish and tadpoles as well as large insects. **Whirligig Beetles (60)** spin about the surface in search of tiny prey. Among the most numerous insects in the pond are the aquatic larvae of flying insects. Shown here are mosquito larvae and a mosquito pupa, a dragonfly nymph, a phantom midge larva, and a mayfly larva.

21

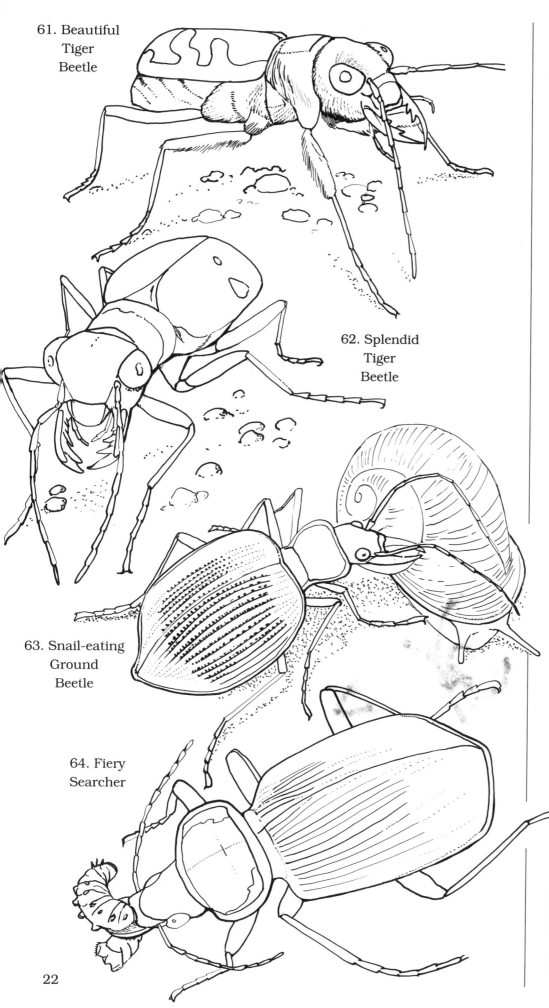

61. Beautiful
Tiger
Beetle

62. Splendid
Tiger
Beetle

63. Snail-eating
Ground
Beetle

64. Fiery
Searcher

## Beetles (Coleoptera)

*There are more kinds of beetles in the world than all other animals combined. Their success comes from their ability to live in almost every kind of habitat, doing all kinds of jobs in nature — beetles are predators, scavengers, plant eaters and suckers, recyclers, even parasites. You can tell them by the line straight down their backs, where their hard, colorful wing-covers meet. Underneath are the clear flying wings. Beetles have complete metamorphosis, in which the larvae (called grubs) are unlike the adults and must pupate to mature.*

### Beautiful Tiger Beetle (61)
Tiger beetles love sandy places where they can hunt small insects. Their iridescent colors show off as they skitter, running and flying, over the ground. This big, bright species lives across much of North America.

### Splendid Tiger Beetle (62)
This striking beetle can be either metallic red or green with sapphire blue rims. It prefers piney woodlands with sandy soil, where its larvae hide in burrows and ambush small prey passing by.

### Snail-eating Ground Beetle
(63) Many of the shiny black beetles you see are ground beetles. This type has a long, narrow thorax and head in order to reach up inside the shells of snails. Look for them where snails and slugs live, in moist green ravines.

### Fiery Searcher (64) Few bee-
tles are more impressive than this brilliant, shiny predator. Because it feeds on the larvae of other insects it is also known as the Caterpillar Hunter. This makes it popular with knowledgeable farmers and gardeners throughout its broad North American range.

**Sexton Beetle (65)** These colorful creatures feed on dead animals, burying their bodies so that other scavengers can't get to them. Their scientific name, *Nicrophorus investigator,* means a discoverer of dead things to eat.

**Northern Carrion Beetle (66)** Carrion beetles lay their eggs in dead bodies; when their grubs hatch, they eat the decomposing flesh and other insects doing the same. These beetles tend to carry a foul stench with them, so you can often smell them before you see them.

**Pictured Rove Beetle (67)** Rove beetles are distinctive, with their very short wing-covers. Their larvae resemble the adults more than those of most other beetles. This kind lives along West Coast beaches, preying on sand fleas.

**Violet Rove Beetle (68)** Basically black, the Violet Rove Beetle shines bright purple-blue in direct light. Although it likes to feed on mushrooms and other fungi, you might have to lift logs and stones to find it. This is always a good technique for beetle-spotting, but be sure to replace their homes!

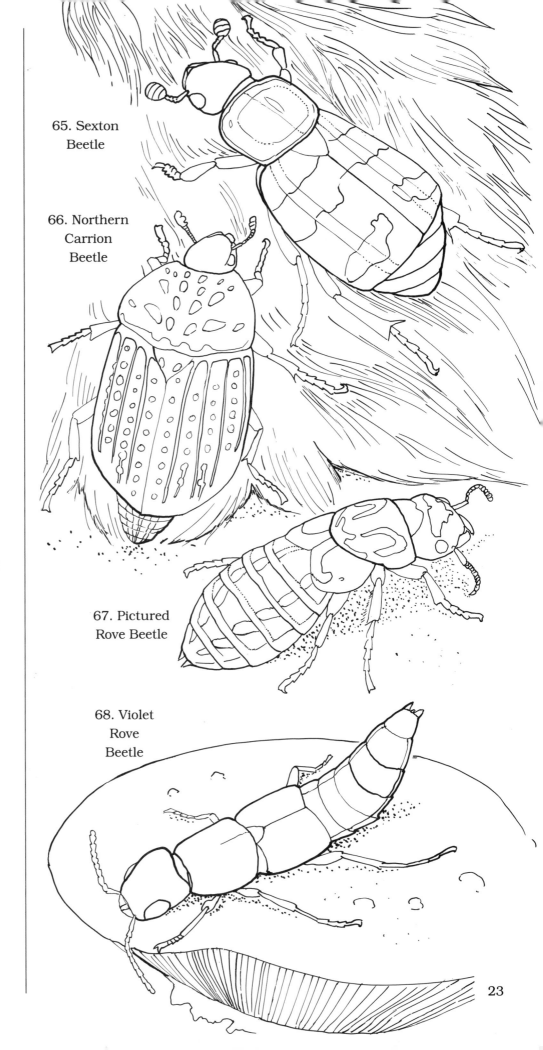

65. Sexton Beetle

66. Northern Carrion Beetle

67. Pictured Rove Beetle

68. Violet Rove Beetle

23

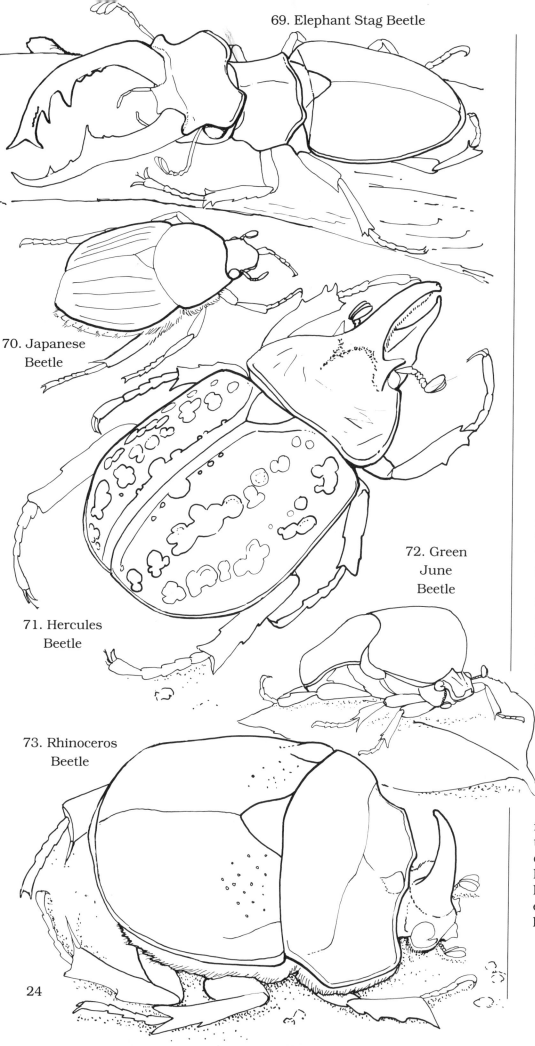

## 69. Elephant Stag Beetle

70. Japanese Beetle

71. Hercules Beetle

72. Green June Beetle

73. Rhinoceros Beetle

**Elephant Stag Beetle (69)** A southeastern woodland species, this is our biggest stag beetle. Males use their impressive "antlers" to fight for the right to mate with females. The grubs feed on rotting wood, while adults lap honeydew, sap, or nectar. Sometimes they fly to lights, startling homeowners.

**Japanese Beetle (70)** Although attractive, Japanese Beetles have not been a welcome addition to the U.S. beetle fauna. The adults feed on a wide variety of desirable plants, and the larvae feed on lawns. Since they were accidentally imported in 1916, they have spread up and down much of the eastern seaboard.

**Hercules Beetle (71)** A southeastern native, this is one of our heaviest beetles, and its tropical relatives are among the world's most massive insects. They sometimes crash into lighted windows at night. This native Hercules likes rotting pines, where its larvae recycle decaying wood.

**Green June Beetle (72)** The adults feed on fruits and flowers, buzzing noisily from one to another. Their grubs consume roots, sometimes becoming pests but aiding public health by attacking the tobacco crop. They look like flying emeralds.

**Rhinoceros Beetle (73)** Like many of the large, horned scarabs and lucanids (stag beetles), these impressive insects are desirable to collectors and sometimes may be overcollected. If you should happen to find one, it is best to leave it. They occur in the eastern states, and only the males have big horns.

**Flower Beetle (74)** These furry beetles with short wing-covers feed on flower pollen, and their grubs eat rotting wood. Like the other beetles on this page, they are in the large and varied family of the scarabs, members of which were sacred to the ancient Egyptians.

**Dung-roller Scarab (75)** Pairs of dung-rollers, or tumble-bugs, roll bits of dung into balls and bury them. Then the female lays her eggs in the ball and the grubs feed on it. They are extemely important in recycling the manure of grazing animals into soil. Egyptian scarab jewelry often depicts dung-rollers.

**Rain Beetle (76)** Confined to the West, these autumn-flying beetles don't feed as adults. The larvae, feeding on roots, may take 10 years or more to develop. When the adult males emerge, they fly to the burrows of flightless females after evening rains.

**Ten-lined Giant Chafer (77)** When big chafers, or June beetles, come to lighted windows at night, they bounce loudly off the panes. The large antennae of the males stand out on this species of the West, where the adults feed on conifers and the grubs feed on roots.

**Beyer's Scarab (78)** With its emerald wing-covers and amethyst legs, this insect is like a living jewel. As a result, it has been overcollected in its few Arizona habitats. If you are lucky enough to see it, just look and don't collect.

**Glorious Scarab (79)** A denizen of juniper canyons in the Southwest, the Glorious Scarab is often thought to be our most beautiful beetle. Like Beyer's Scarab, it is endangered and should be appreciated without being collected.

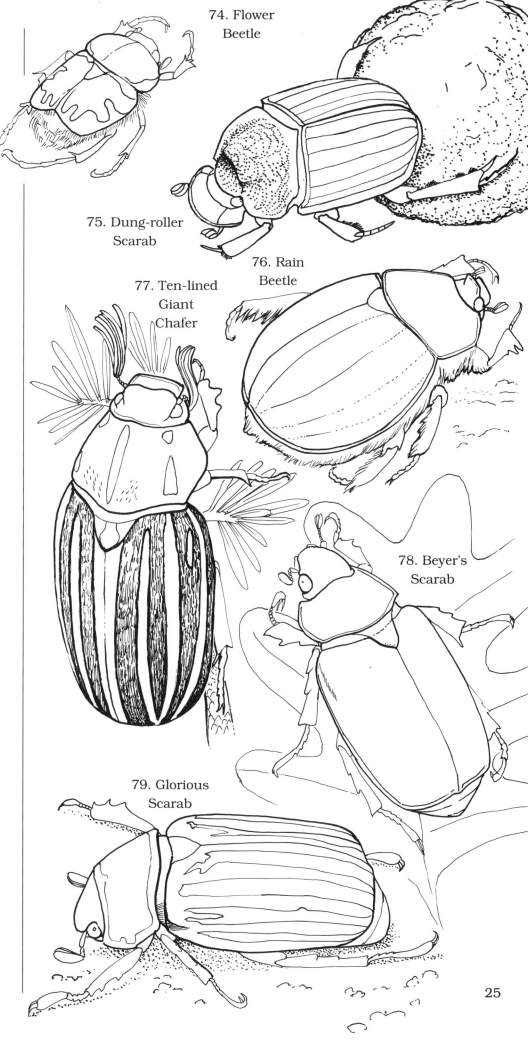

74. Flower Beetle

75. Dung-roller Scarab

76. Rain Beetle

77. Ten-lined Giant Chafer

78. Beyer's Scarab

79. Glorious Scarab

25

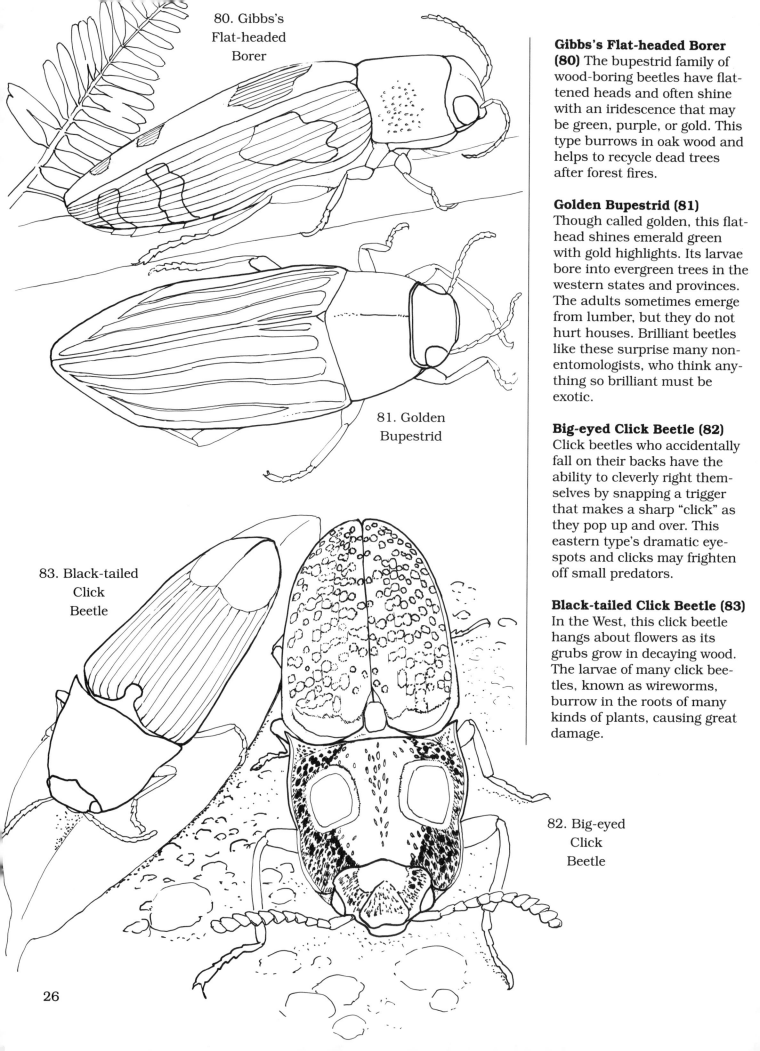

### 80. Gibbs's Flat-headed Borer

### 81. Golden Bupestrid

### 83. Black-tailed Click Beetle

### 82. Big-eyed Click Beetle

**Gibbs's Flat-headed Borer (80)** The bupestrid family of wood-boring beetles have flattened heads and often shine with an iridescence that may be green, purple, or gold. This type burrows in oak wood and helps to recycle dead trees after forest fires.

**Golden Bupestrid (81)** Though called golden, this flathead shines emerald green with gold highlights. Its larvae bore into evergreen trees in the western states and provinces. The adults sometimes emerge from lumber, but they do not hurt houses. Brilliant beetles like these surprise many non-entomologists, who think anything so brilliant must be exotic.

**Big-eyed Click Beetle (82)** Click beetles who accidentally fall on their backs have the ability to cleverly right themselves by snapping a trigger that makes a sharp "click" as they pop up and over. This eastern type's dramatic eyespots and clicks may frighten off small predators.

**Black-tailed Click Beetle (83)** In the West, this click beetle hangs about flowers as its grubs grow in decaying wood. The larvae of many click beetles, known as wireworms, burrow in the roots of many kinds of plants, causing great damage.

**Pennsylvania Firefly (84)**
Fireflies, or lightning bugs, belong to a family called Lampyridae — meaning "fire lamp." They and their larvae have the remarkable ability to generate a glowing green or yellow light from their bodies. They flash their lamps to one another in a courtship code, lighting up eastern summer nights.

**Goldenrod Soldier Beetle (85)** Soldier beetles have narrow, leathery wings and long bodies. Their bright colors and large numbers make them stand out on the flowers they love to visit for pollen. Their grubs are helpful predators of other insects.

**Net-winged Beetle (86)** Their wide, rounded wing-covers with a netlike pattern of ridges help you to identify these unusual beetles. They feed on decaying plant material in eastern woods and meadows. Certain moths have similar patterns and colors, probably because the beetles, the moths, or both are distasteful to birds, who learn to leave alone all insects that look like this.

**Soft-winged Flower Beetle (87)** As you might guess from the name, these are less hard-shelled than many beetles, and the adults visit flowers. Their grubs are predators or scavengers.

**California Checkered Beetle (88)** Checkered beetles have the strange habit of mating while the female sucks the bodily juices of a caterpillar. Since the adults feed on moth larvae and the grubs eat grasshopper eggs, these are popular beetles with farmers who know them.

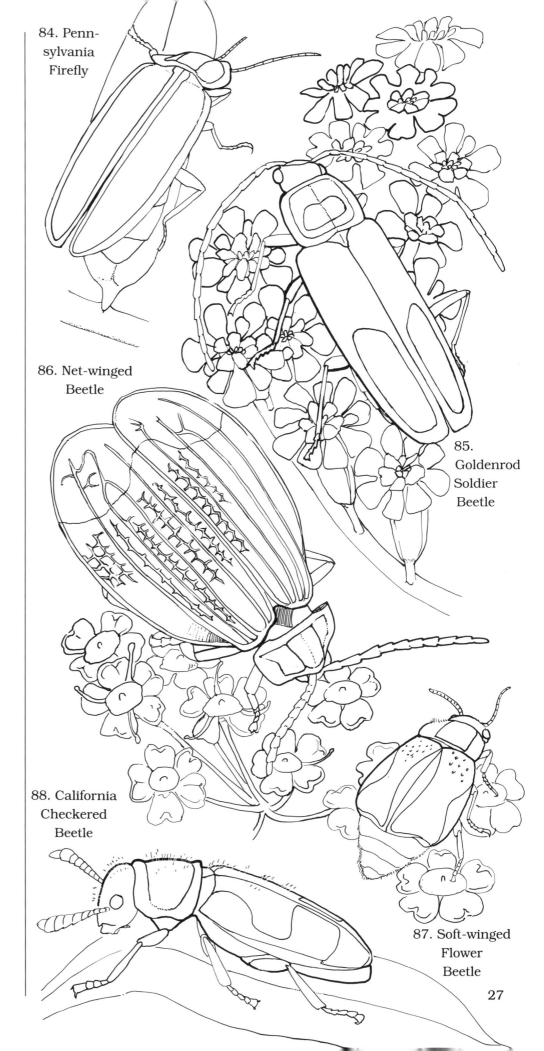

84. Pennsylvania Firefly

86. Net-winged Beetle

85. Goldenrod Soldier Beetle

88. California Checkered Beetle

87. Soft-winged Flower Beetle

27

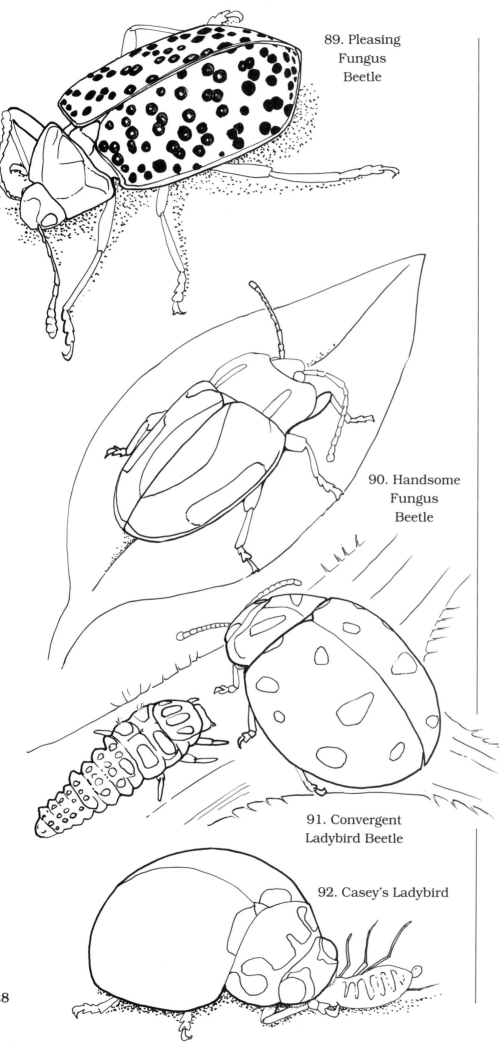

89. Pleasing Fungus Beetle

90. Handsome Fungus Beetle

91. Convergent Ladybird Beetle

92. Casey's Ladybird

**Pleasing Fungus Beetle (89)** Both the larvae and adults of this Rocky Mountain species like mushrooms, though the beetles may be found on flowers too. Other members of this colorful family specialize on fungi such as shelf conchs and molds.

**Handsome Fungus Beetle (90)** Another fungi-feeding family, also attractive, these beetles are not common. Sometimes they spend the winter in groups beneath organic matter on the ground. This species has distinctive horns at the front edge of its thorax.

**Convergent Ladybird Beetle (91)** Ladybird beetles, often called "ladybugs," are among everyone's favorite insects. Not only are they helpful in consuming unwanted insects in the garden, but they are pretty and seem to be friendly. Sometimes they hibernate in enormous numbers, gathering in great orange patches on rocks and tree trunks before they take shelter from freezing temperatures. Its larva is shown here too.

**Casey's Ladybird (92)** Ladybird beetles come with many different spot patterns; this kind has no black spots on its wing cases. It lives in the western states. Both the adult and larval stages of ladybirds are beneficial, consuming billions of aphids, so they are often imported into gardens.

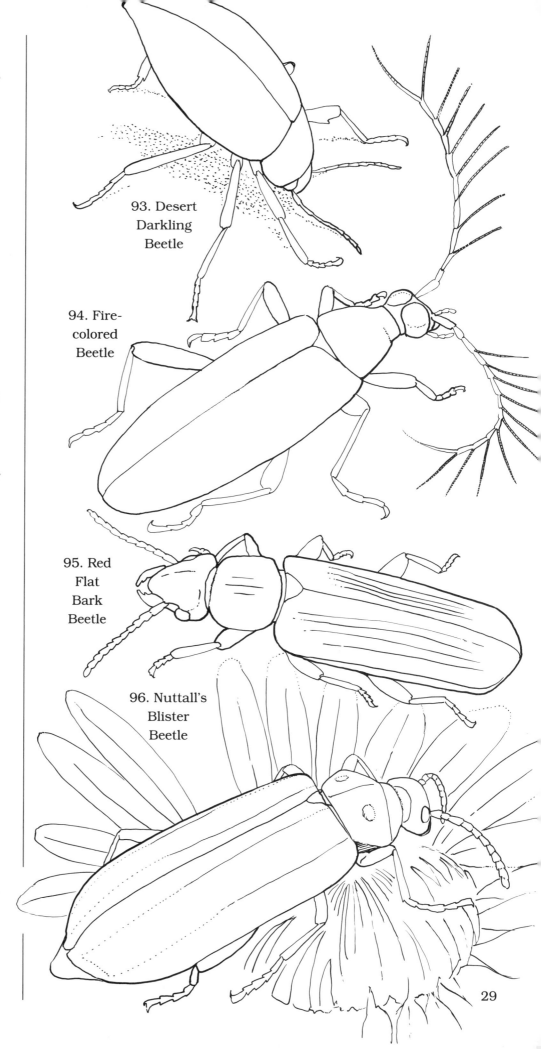

## Desert Darkling Beetle (93)

Also known as skunk beetles, darklings stand on their heads when irritated and expel a strong, repellent odor. This sometimes saves them from predators. Both adults and grubs once fed on native prairie grasses; now that the prairies have been plowed, they feed on grains and other crops.

## Fire-colored Beetle (94)

These are recognized by their flaming red color, big eyes, and bizarre, branched antennae. They may be drawn to lights at night, for they are largely nocturnal. They often spend days under bark or logs, where the larvae feed on smaller insects, then come out at night to visit flowers.

## Red Flat Bark Beetle (95)

Very flat and very red, this eye-opening beetle is a familiar sight to woodcutters. The larvae hunt the grubs of other beetles beneath the bark of hardwoods, where the adults are likely to be found as well. They are so flat that they can squeeze into remarkably tight spaces under bark.

## Nuttall's Blister Beetle (96)

This magnificent big beetle shows brilliant iridescence ranging from bluish black through purple, red, green, and gold. It occurs in great colonies in Rocky Mountain flower meadows, where about half the population seems to be mating at any one time. The females are considerably larger than the males, as they must produce many eggs. When disturbed, blister beetles leak blood that can be very irritating to the skin. Adults feed on flowers, but larvae live in bee nests.

93. Desert Darkling Beetle

94. Fire-colored Beetle

95. Red Flat Bark Beetle

96. Nuttall's Blister Beetle

29

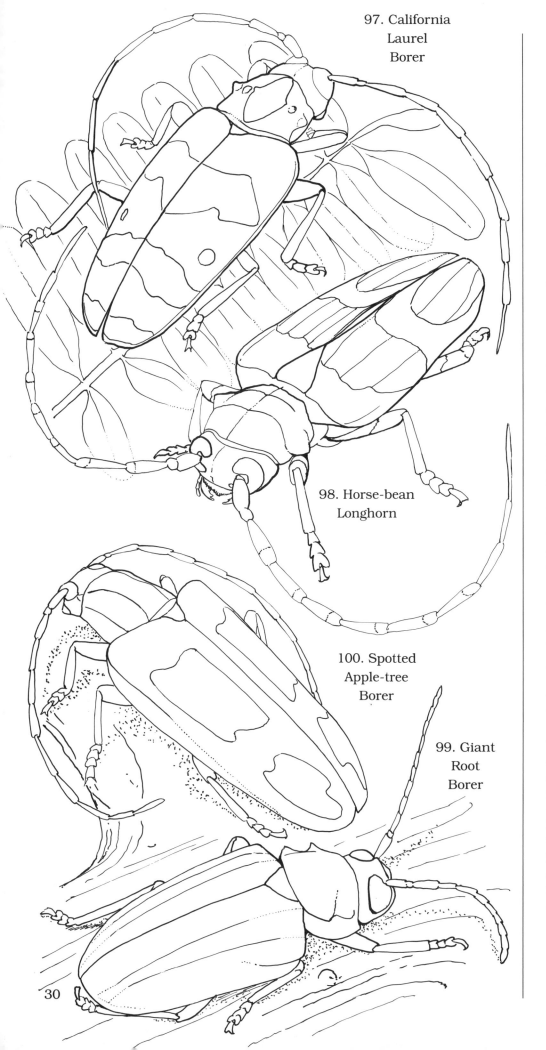

97. California
Laurel
Borer

98. Horse-bean
Longhorn

100. Spotted
Apple-tree
Borer

99. Giant
Root
Borer

30

**California Laurel Borer (97)**
Longhorn wood-boring beetles are known by their extremely long antennae, with which they feel about in wood to lay their eggs. The bluish white and black Laurel Borer is one of the most handsome of all western beetles. When people see it they think it must be rare, but it is common in much of the West around laurel, ash, alder, and willow.

**Horse-bean Longhorn (98)**
Another very dramatic longhorn, this one occupies the Southwest. Its great beauty delights those who see it, but does not impress the citrus growers whose trees it eats.

**Giant Root Borer (99)** Species of these big beetles range through much of the continent. The larvae eat the roots of a wide variety of woody plants. Adults often fly to lights at night, and if you think a rock has hit your window, it might be one of these. Some of their relatives hang out about firs, pines, and telephone poles.

**Spotted Apple-tree Borer (100)** The adults feed on foliage and twigs, while their larvae bore into the inner bark and sapwood — often in the same trees. They are by no means restricted to apple trees, however. These beetles are favorites with collectors, but being shy and alert, they quickly fly when approached. Some longhorns serve as very important pollinators of flowers. For example, the related **Red Milkweed Longhorn Beetle** both feeds on and pollinates its host plants. Look for a mating pair in the milkweed meadow scene shown on page 33.

**Golden Tortoise Beetle (101)**
This turtle-shaped insect
resembles a drop of molten
gold when it is living, but the
gilding fades upon death. It
has a clear, glassy, flat rim
around the edge. Its beauty
helps to make up for the holes
it chews in morning glories.

**Dogbane Beetle (102)** These
bright beetles cluster on dogbane and related plants,
where larvae feed below
ground, adults above. Their
greeny-copper iridescence
makes you want to touch
them, but when disturbed
they drop to the ground and
stink. This is an eastern animal, but a related blue species
occurs in the West.

**Sunflower Beetle (103)** Like
the other beetles on this page,
this attractive insect belongs
to a big family called the leaf
beetles. Rounded, stripy beetles on sunflowers are likely
this species.

**Calligraphy Beetle (104)** Its
scientific name, *Calligrapha
serpentina*, means "snaky
writing." This strongly pat-
terned animal lives in the
Southwest but has similar relatives in other regions. Adults
and grubs feed on various
trees and shrubs.

**Spotted Cucumber Beetle
(105)** With the adults chewing
up the leaves of cucumbers
and the larvae ruining the
roots of corn and other crops,
this is not a favorite of farmers. It transmits bacteria that
wilt crops and is also known
as the Southern Corn Root-
worm.

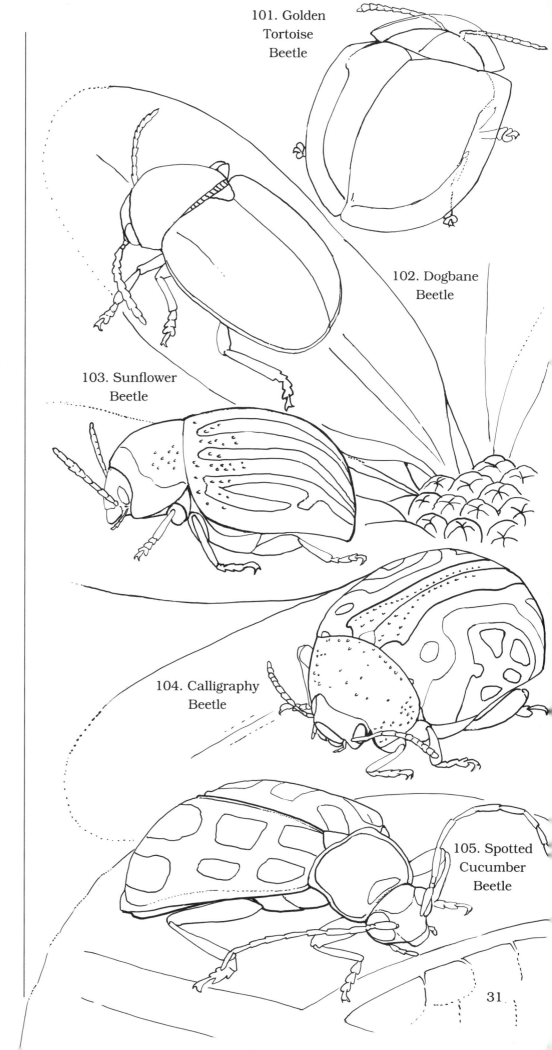

101. Golden
Tortoise
Beetle

102. Dogbane
Beetle

103. Sunflower
Beetle

104. Calligraphy
Beetle

105. Spotted
Cucumber
Beetle

31

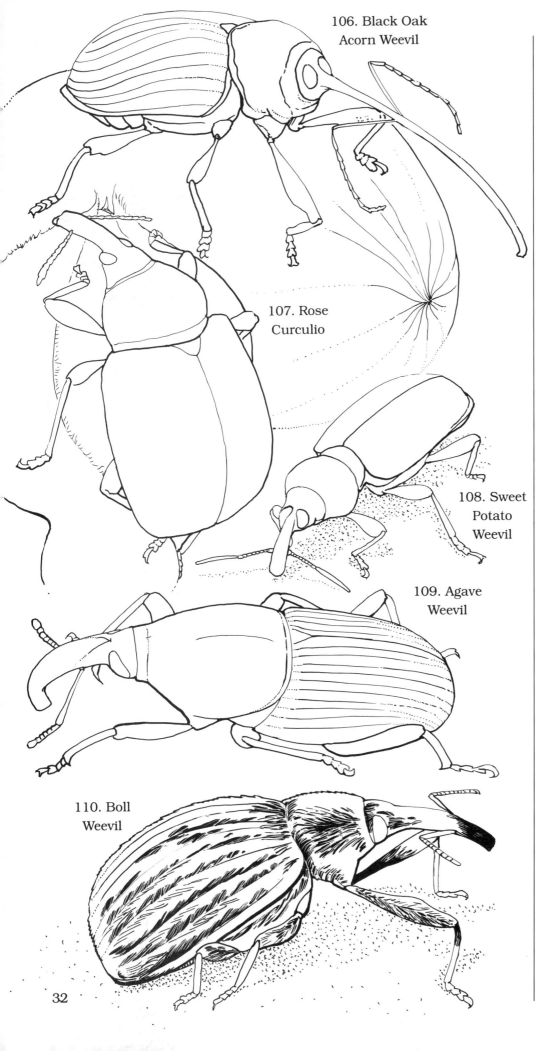

106. Black Oak
Acorn Weevil

107. Rose
Curculio

108. Sweet
Potato
Weevil

109. Agave
Weevil

110. Boll
Weevil

32

**Black Oak Acorn Weevil (106)**
This page shows weevils, the largest family of beetles, with over 2,500 species in North America and many times that in the world. They have sucking beaks and are also called snout beetles. This species bores into acorns and lays its eggs there; later the larvae eat out the flesh.

**Rose Curculio (107)** In thickets of wild rose, these pretty rose-red weevils may appear on almost every pink and yellow blossom. Rather than sucking, they have chewing mouthparts at the end of their long snout. After they eat the seeds, they lay their eggs in rose hips, which the larvae consume.

**Sweet Potato Weevil (108)**
This small, orange and blue weevil looks like a bright rubber ant in unlikely colors. Unfortunately, sweet potato farmers cannot appreciate it because of the great damage weevils do to their crop.

**Agave Weevil (109)** Notice how these weevils have their antennae attached to their snouts instead of their foreheads. This sturdy black beetle of the Southwest feeds on agaves, big thick spiky plants from which a kind of beer is made in Mexico.

**Boll Weevil (110)** This is one of the few beetles (along with the ladybird) to have a song written about it. It has affected the lives of many people by spoiling vast quantities of cotton before it can be harvested. Both adults and grubs feed on the bolls, or developing flowers of cotton. They arrived from Mexico a century ago and have baffled entomologists ever since.

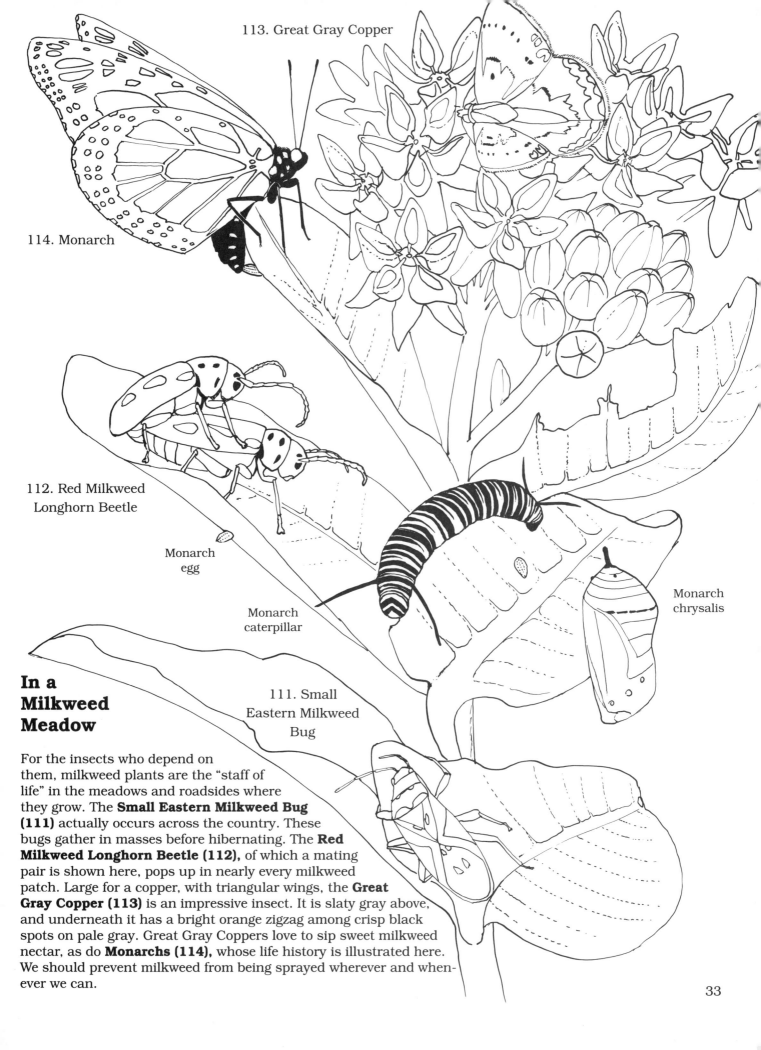

113. Great Gray Copper

114. Monarch

112. Red Milkweed
Longhorn Beetle

Monarch
egg

Monarch
caterpillar

Monarch
chrysalis

111. Small
Eastern Milkweed
Bug

## In a Milkweed Meadow

For the insects who depend on them, milkweed plants are the "staff of life" in the meadows and roadsides where they grow. The **Small Eastern Milkweed Bug (111)** actually occurs across the country. These bugs gather in masses before hibernating. The **Red Milkweed Longhorn Beetle (112),** of which a mating pair is shown here, pops up in nearly every milkweed patch. Large for a copper, with triangular wings, the **Great Gray Copper (113)** is an impressive insect. It is slaty gray above, and underneath it has a bright orange zigzag among crisp black spots on pale gray. Great Gray Coppers love to sip sweet milkweed nectar, as do **Monarchs (114),** whose life history is illustrated here. We should prevent milkweed from being sprayed wherever and whenever we can.

33

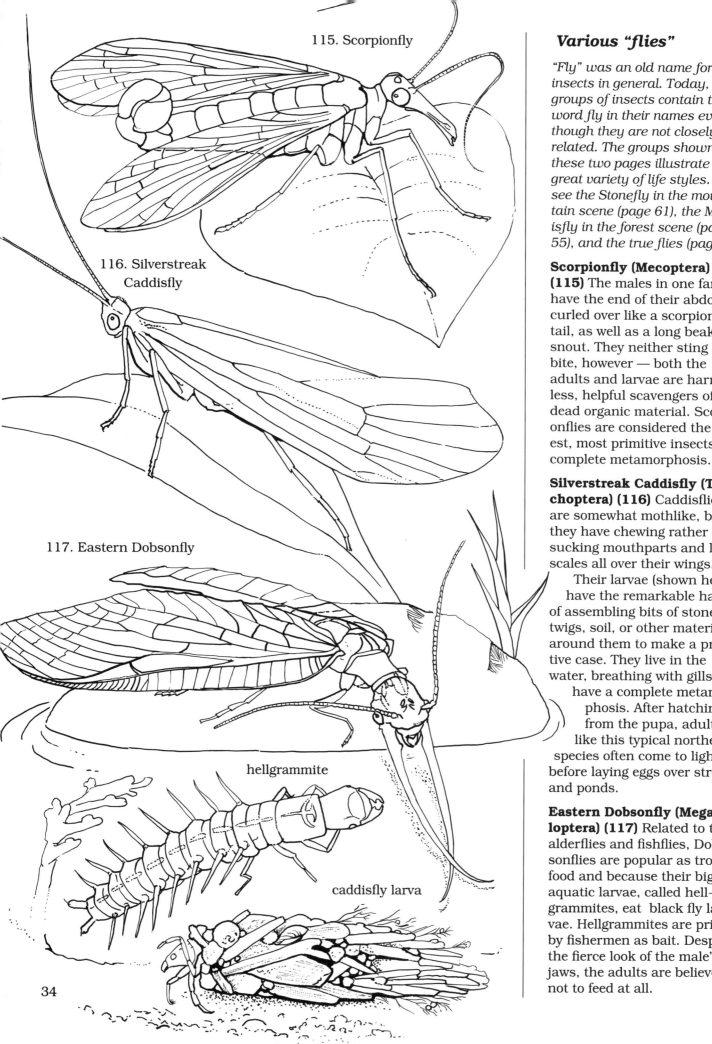

115. Scorpionfly

116. Silverstreak Caddisfly

117. Eastern Dobsonfly

hellgrammite

caddisfly larva

## Various "flies"

*"Fly" was an old name for insects in general. Today, many groups of insects contain the word fly in their names even though they are not closely related. The groups shown on these two pages illustrate a great variety of life styles. Also see the Stonefly in the mountain scene (page 61), the Mantisfly in the forest scene (page 55), and the true flies (page 62).*

**Scorpionfly (Mecoptera) (115)** The males in one family have the end of their abdomen curled over like a scorpion's tail, as well as a long beaklike snout. They neither sting nor bite, however — both the adults and larvae are harmless, helpful scavengers of dead organic material. Scorpionflies are considered the oldest, most primitive insects with complete metamorphosis.

**Silverstreak Caddisfly (Trichoptera) (116)** Caddisflies are somewhat mothlike, but they have chewing rather than sucking mouthparts and lack scales all over their wings.

Their larvae (shown here) have the remarkable habit of assembling bits of stone, twigs, soil, or other material around them to make a protective case. They live in the water, breathing with gills, and have a complete metamorphosis. After hatching from the pupa, adults like this typical northern species often come to lights before laying eggs over streams and ponds.

**Eastern Dobsonfly (Megaloptera) (117)** Related to the alderflies and fishflies, Dobsonflies are popular as trout food and because their big aquatic larvae, called hellgrammites, eat black fly larvae. Hellgrammites are prized by fishermen as bait. Despite the fierce look of the male's big jaws, the adults are believed not to feed at all.

34

## Golden Mayfly (Ephemeroptera) (118)

Mayflies emerge in spring to fly in mating clouds over water. After mating, they live for only a few hours or days. They are known by their trim form, long tail filaments, and shiny net-veined wings. The adults don't feed, but the larvae prey on tiny animals and algae.

## Green Lacewing (Neuroptera) (119)

Jade green with brilliant golden eyes, lacewings are a familiar sight on a summer's evening in meadows or woods. Both the adults and larvae are considered beneficial, since they feed on mealybugs and aphids. They are not always pleasant to be around, however, since they can give a little nip and give off a sharp odor of mothballs.

## Texas Snakefly (Rhaphidioptera) (120)

These peculiar insects resemble lacewings, but the females have long ovipositors (egg-layers), and their necks stretch out and up in a snakelike pose. The young change completely, and like the adults prey on other insects. Only about 20 kinds of snakeflies live in North America, all in the West.

## Antlion (121)

Antlions, like lacewings, belong to the Neuroptera, or nerve-winged insects, so named for their network of wing veins. Many people mistake the flower-visiting adults for damselflies, but their short, clubbed antennae give them away. The larva (pictured below the adult) is the famous "doodlebug," which lies buried in wait at the bottom of a sandpit with only its fierce jaws showing. Ants and other small creatures tumble down into the pit and don't have a chance.

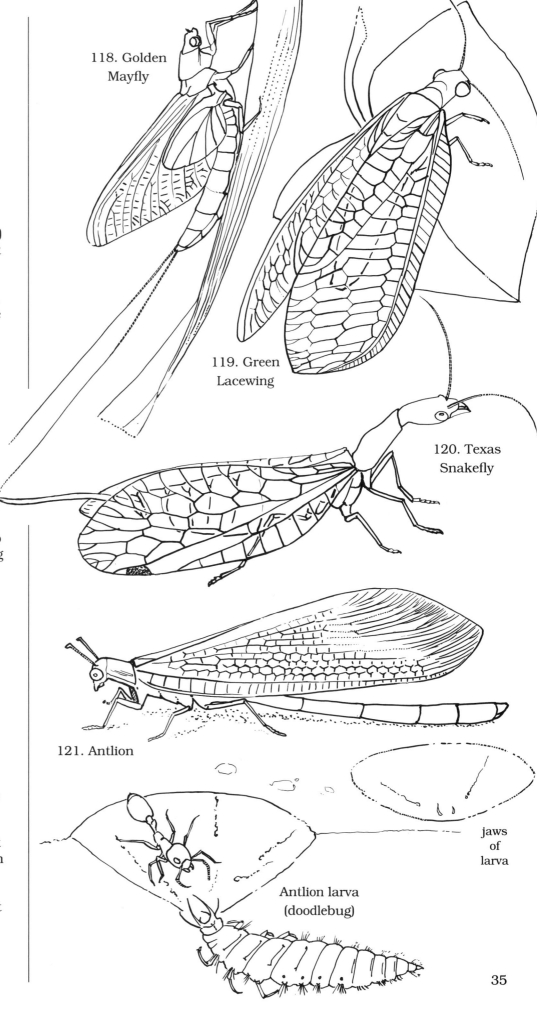

118. Golden Mayfly

119. Green Lacewing

120. Texas Snakefly

121. Antlion

jaws of larva

Antlion larva (doodlebug)

35

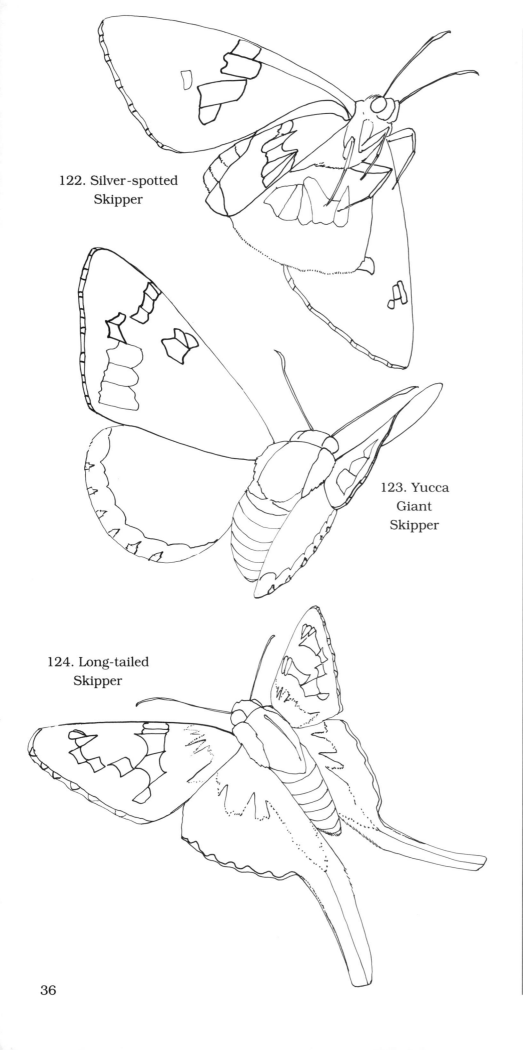

**122. Silver-spotted Skipper**

**123. Yucca Giant Skipper**

**124. Long-tailed Skipper**

## Butterflies and Moths (Lepidoptera)

*By far the best known of all insects, as well as the best loved, butterflies and moths are also some of the most advanced of the arthropods. They have scales covering their wings like tiny shingles, sucking mouthparts like a drinking straw that they can coil when not in use, and a complete metamorphosis with egg, caterpillar, chrysalis, and adult stages. Of some 20,000 butterflies in the world, around 700 live in North America. In any given place, moths outnumber butterflies at a rate of between 10 and 100 to one, both in species and in individuals. Moths lack the clubbed antennae that all butterflies have.*

**Silver-spotted Skipper (122)**
A frequent garden visitor, this big skipper likes honeysuckle both for nectar and to lay its eggs on. Its large silver and gold patches are almost alarming in flight as it flashes past. Skippers are a family of butterflies with hooked antennae and strong, stout bodies.

**Yucca Giant Skipper (123)**
Giant skippers are even bigger than the Silver-spotted, up to three inches in wingspan. Their powerful flight muscles allow them to fly 60 miles an hour or more. Their big caterpillars bore into the roots of yuccas and agaves across the southern states and into Mexico.

**Long-tailed Skipper (124)**
Throughout the South you may see this impressive skipper all year long during mild weather. It loves to visit lantana and other flowers, quivering its tailed wings as it sips nectar, its body fur shimmering blue in the sunshine. Sometimes it migrates to new territory in huge numbers.

**Arctic Skipper (125)** A very pretty skipper with golden yellow and silvery spots on its short wings. It is not called "arctic" because it lives only in the Far North but because it ranges around the Northern Hemisphere in cool climates. As it hangs from flowers in early morning, its spots resemble dewdrops.

**Delaware Skipper (126)** There are many species of tawny little skippers, of which this is one of the brightest. They are commonly called the "golden grass skippers" because their caterpillars all feed on grasses, and they are found in prairies and lawns that have not been sprayed. Every region has one or more kinds of tawny lawn skippers to brighten butterfly gardens in midsummer. The Delaware may be found along watercourses in the eastern half of the country.

**Zabulon Skipper (127)** Like the other small grass skippers, these hold their hindwings and forewings at different angles when they open them. Many, including this species, are named for eastern Native Americans. The male and female are very different in coloration, a trait known as sexual dimorphism.

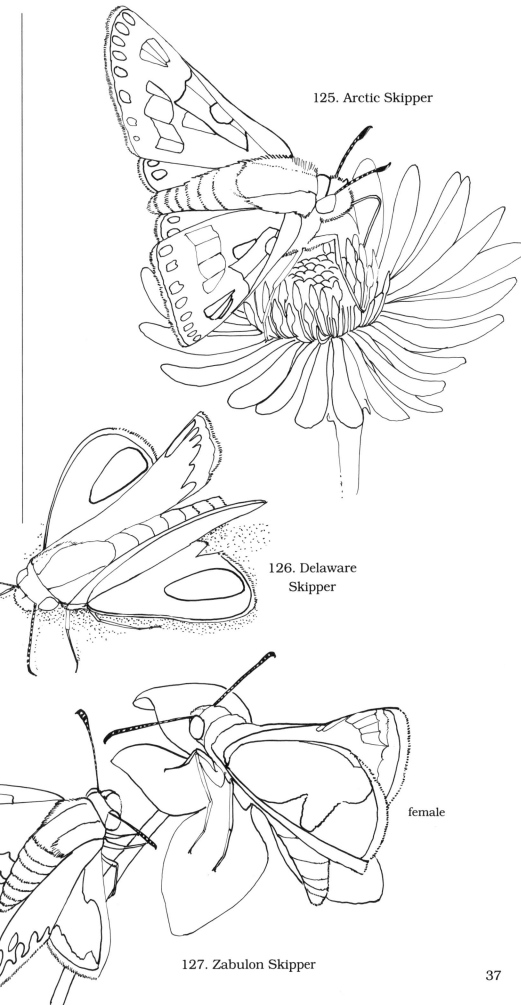

125. Arctic Skipper

126. Delaware Skipper

female

male

127. Zabulon Skipper

37

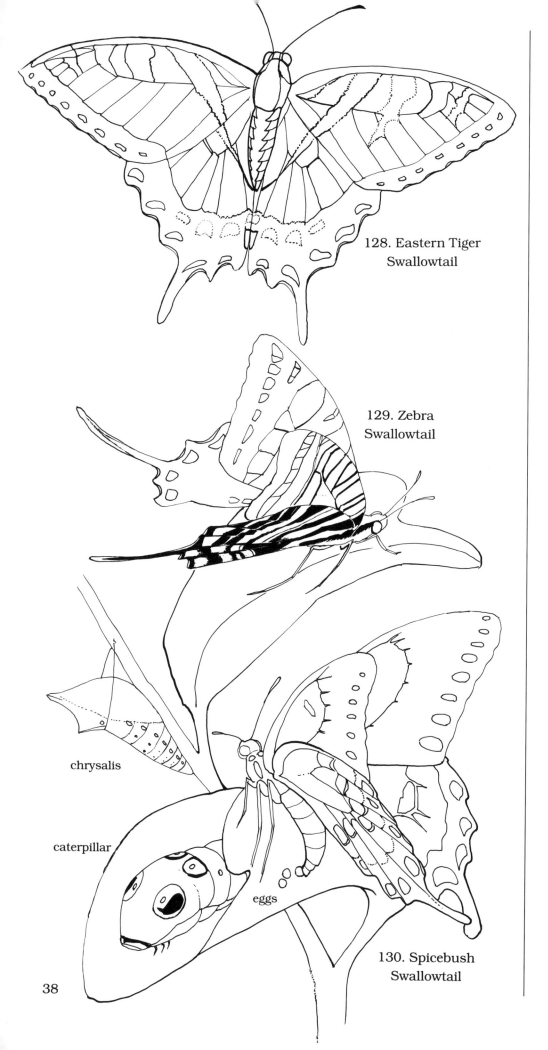

128. Eastern Tiger Swallowtail

129. Zebra Swallowtail

chrysalis

caterpillar

eggs

130. Spicebush Swallowtail

38

## Eastern Tiger Swallowtail (128)
While skippers are among our smallest butterflies, swallowtails are the largest. Almost everyone knows the big yellow sailors known as tiger swallowtails. This one lives in eastern cities and woods, but a similar species occupies the West and another the northland. Their caterpillars feed on willows, cherries, and other broad-leafed trees, but never enough to be pests. On the contrary, their beauty is a great addition to our cities and gardens.

## Zebra Swallowtail (129)
A most elegant creature, the Zebra Swallowtail sports very long, sleek tails and fine black and red racing stripes. Their larvae eat only pawpaw, a bush or tree of rural areas, so they tend to disappear where too much development occurs. You can encourage them by planting pawpaw as well as the nectar plants they prefer, such as phlox and asters.

## Spicebush Swallowtail (130)
The caterpillars of many butterflies will eat only certain kinds of plants. This beautiful black butterfly with blue, green, yellow, and orange markings feeds on spicebush, sassafras, and bay in its larval stage. Note and color its full life history on this page, and compare the stages with those of the Pipevine Swallowtail on the next. Adults are less picky than the larvae, drinking nectar from many kinds of flowers, but Green Swallowtails (as these are also called) have a special liking for pickerelweed.

**Pipevine Swallowtail (131)**
You'll never forget the first time you see *philenor* (its attractive Latin name). This big, brilliant butterfly shimmers like blue mylar on its upper side, and flashes fire-engine red spots beneath. The bright colors advertise to birds the toxic qualities it gets from feeding on poisonous pipevine as a caterpillar. The striking red and black larva is distasteful, too. Notice the silken girdle by which the swallowtail chrysalis hangs. See page 44 for two other butterflies that mimic this one, fooling birds into leaving them alone.

**Giant Swallowtail (132)** The biggest butterfly in North America lives in the South, where it sails over many kinds of habitats. Its caterpillars, which look like big bird droppings, are known as "orange dogs" because they like to browse on citrus leaves. The tails of swallowtails don't do much to help them fly, but serve as targets to guide bird attacks away from their bodies.

**Phoebus Parnassian (133)** We know that the parnassians are closely related to the swallowtails by the veins of their wings, but they don't look alike. These western mountain butterflies are waxy white with dusky gray and scaleless, transparent patches as well as bright ruby spots. They live on stonecrop plants on the high ridges; one coastal species lives on bleeding-hearts. Phoebus is also called Smintheus, both of which are names for the Greek god Apollo. It will also be found in the mountain scene (page 61).

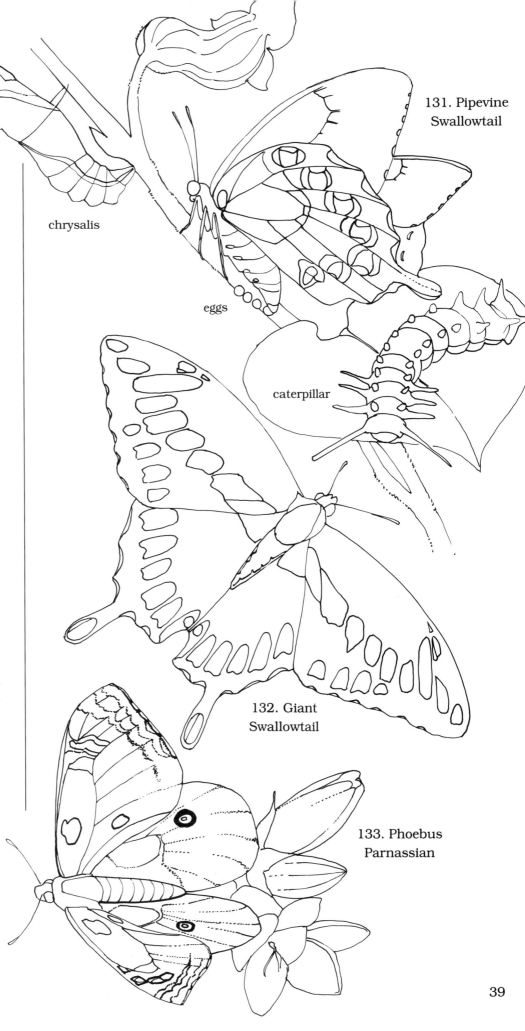

chrysalis

eggs

caterpillar

131. Pipevine Swallowtail

132. Giant Swallowtail

133. Phoebus Parnassian

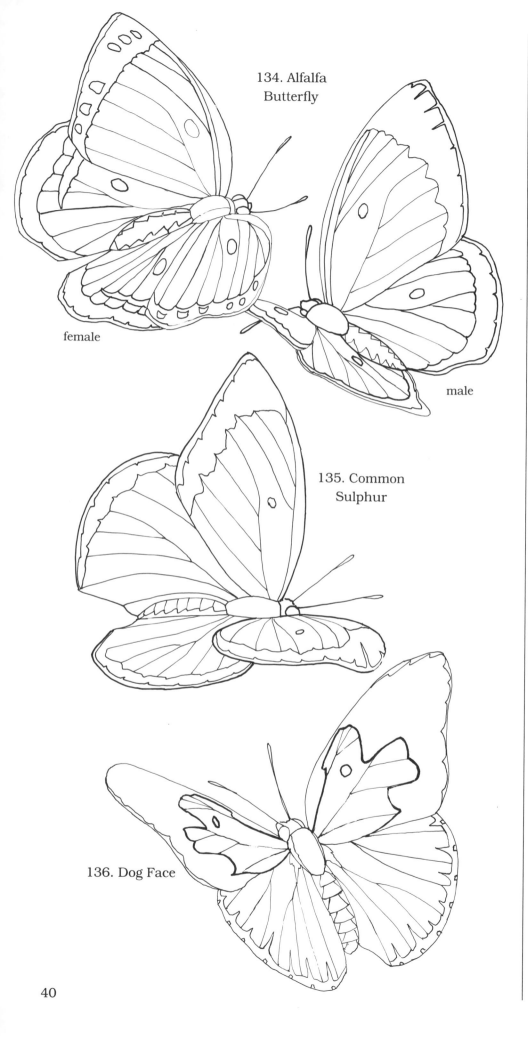

134. Alfalfa Butterfly

female

male

135. Common Sulphur

136. Dog Face

**Alfalfa Butterfly (134)** Also known as the Orange Sulphur, this much-loved American butterfly is exactly the color of a Union Pacific locomotive. The males and females differ in the markings along the edge of the wing, as you can see here. Because it feeds on alfalfa and clover, it has become terrifically abundant in the countryside. Watch for clouds of orange over the alfalfa fields. Sometimes this species interbreeds with the closely related Common Sulphur, making half-orange, half-yellow offspring.

**Common Sulphur (135)** It was an insect like this one that gave the name "butter-fly" to this group of insects. Yellow sulphurs are common across much of the Northern Hemisphere. Their larvae feed on members of the pea family, which grow nearly everywhere. This is one of the most common butterflies in North America. Often, you can see their dancing courtship flights over parks, gardens, and fields. Hay farmers do not share the popular affection for these bright butterflies, since their green caterpillars gobble their crops.

**Dog Face (136)** Can you spot the poodle head on the forewings of this butterfly? The Dog Face really stands out when it spreads its wings, but it blends into the undergrowth when the greenish underside shows. In winter broods, the underside is rosy. The related California Dog Face, or Flying Pansy, looks very similar, but it has orange hindwings and a purple flush over the poodle. It is the official California state insect.

**Orange-barred Sulphur (137)**
Giant sulphurs fly throughout the world's tropical regions. This one lives in Florida and Texas and south from there. Its strong orange bands across bright yellow wings are distinctive, if it ever sits still long enough for you to see those marks. The related Cloudless Giant Sulphur is the big "buttery fly" that people commonly see throughout the South and up and down the East Coast, sometimes in mass migrations.

**Sara's Orangetip (138)** This spring butterfly, like other kinds of orangetips, looks like two bits of orange flickering through the air all by themselves. The caterpillar's food plants include ladies' smocks and wild mustards, so watch for them around these plants near streams, waterfalls, or the edges of woods. Males are white above, females yellow, and both have delicate green marbling below. They are common in the Northwest.

**Olympia Marblewing (139)**
Grassy spots where mustards and cresses grow in the early spring furnish the best conditions for this lovely species. Sometimes there is a simple rosy pattern in the grass green marbling against the white background. Other marblewings occupy the western mountains, but this one ranges into the Great Plains and the Appalachians.

**Terloot's Pine White (140)**
This autumn flier, also known as the Chiricahua Pine White, lives in southern Arizona mountains, where its caterpillars feed on Ponderosa Pine needles. The male and female look very different from each other, the female seeming to mimic toxic orange insects. More often seen is the related Pine White, common across much of the mountainous West.

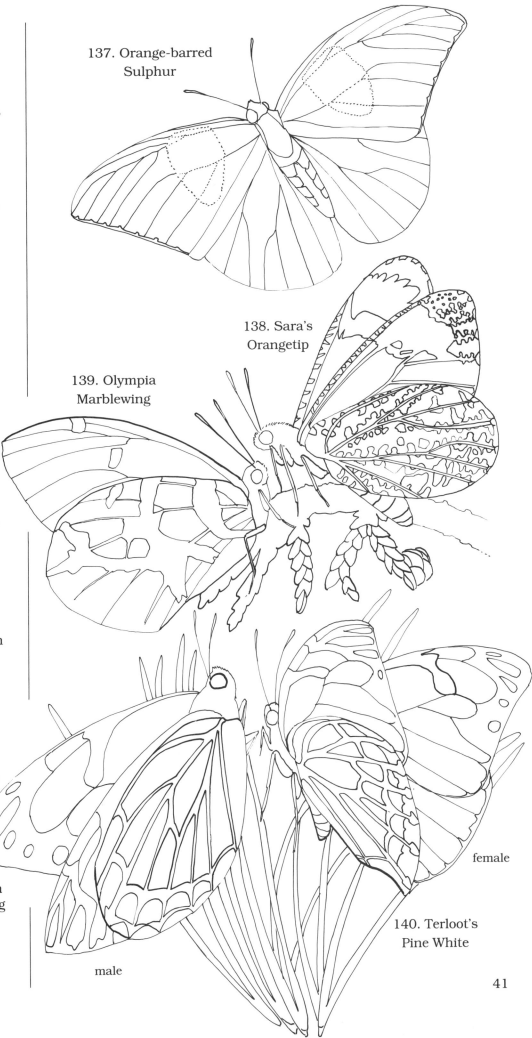

137. Orange-barred Sulphur

138. Sara's Orangetip

139. Olympia Marblewing

female

140. Terloot's Pine White

male

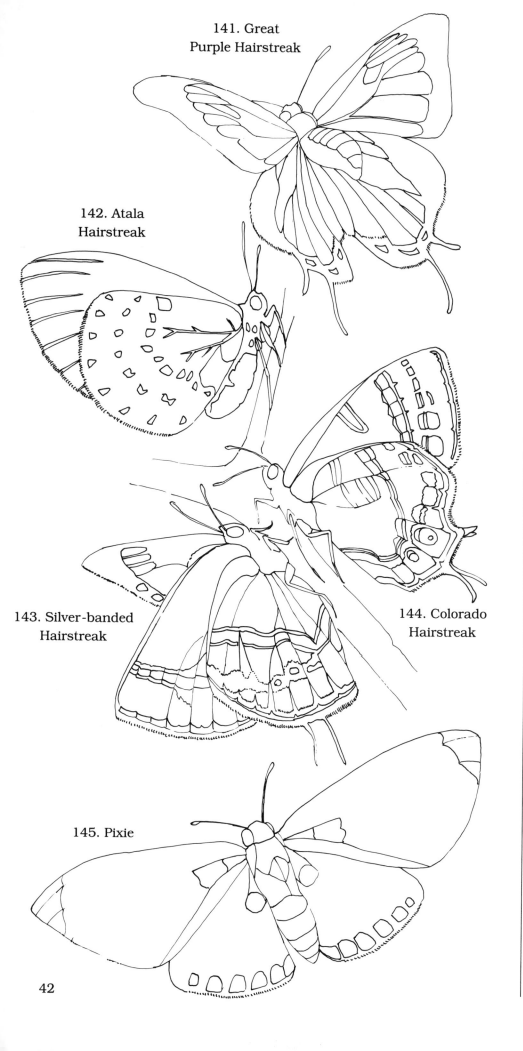

**141. Great Purple Hairstreak**

**142. Atala Hairstreak**

**143. Silver-banded Hairstreak**

**144. Colorado Hairstreak**

**145. Pixie**

**Great Purple Hairstreak (141)** Hairstreaks are named for their streaking flight and for the hairlike tails on the hindwings that lure birds away from their bodies. In spite of its traditional name, this big hairstreak (one inch plus) is actually more iridescent blue than purple. Either way, it is a great representative of the gossamer-winged butterflies, which occupy these two pages. This family contains small, bright, fast butterflies, often with metallic colors. The Great Purple nectars abundantly in southern flowerbeds and vacant lots, but its caterpillars eat mistletoe.

**Atala Hairstreak (142)** Mostly a tropical butterfly of the Caribbean, Atala comes and goes in southern Florida as well. It was once thought extinct, then endangered, but now it is fairly common again. Its caterpillars feed on coontie and taste as bad as the butterflies, who advertise this fact with a bright red spot on their body and wings. Their green scales are like tiny emeralds.

**Silver-banded Hairstreak (143)** Only in the southernmost states might you see this striking species, which is green below, purple above, and has a lightninglike silver slash.

**Colorado Hairstreak (144)** This flying gem plays among the scrub oaks of the southern Rocky Mountains. While the underside is silvery, blue, and orange, the top shows deep amethyst purple. Fourth graders in Colorado are responsible for having it designated as the official state insect.

**Pixie (145)** This Texan insect flies both winter and summer. It is black, with orange wingtips and red spots. Its markings make it a unique member of the group of gossamer-wings known as the metalmarks, most of which are shades of brown. Many colorful relatives of the Pixie live in Latin America.

**Purplish Copper (146)** Wetlands and meadows throughout the West where knotweed and docks grow are likely to have these or related coppers flitting about. The females have brown spots on orange, but the males shine purple if the sun strikes them at the right angle. You can often identify coppers by the orange zigzag on the hindwing.

**American Copper (147)** This tiny butterfly with its contrasting pattern of dark brown and bright, fiery orange is common in the Northeast in a variety of habitats, including vacant lots, but it is rare in the West in high mountain retreats. Although it is called American, it has a very close relative in England and the rest of Europe.

**Eastern Tailed Blue (148)** There is another little lepidopteran called the Western Tailed Blue, which is less heavily spotted. Both kinds feed on clovers and vetches and other pea-family plants, as do many other blues. Like hairstreaks, they have tiny taillike hairs on the hindwings. Silvery Blues, Common Blues, Spring Azures, and many other small blue butterflies congregate around moist spots all over North America, especially in the mountains.

**Sonora Blue (149)** This is the only blue with orange patches on both the forewings and hindwings, and is the brightest of all the blues. The prism-like scales on its wings give it iridescent colors. It feeds on a strange succulent plant called rock lettuce in California canyons, and emerges from its chrysalis as early as January.

146. Purplish Copper

147. American Copper

148. Eastern Tailed Blue

149. Sonora Blue

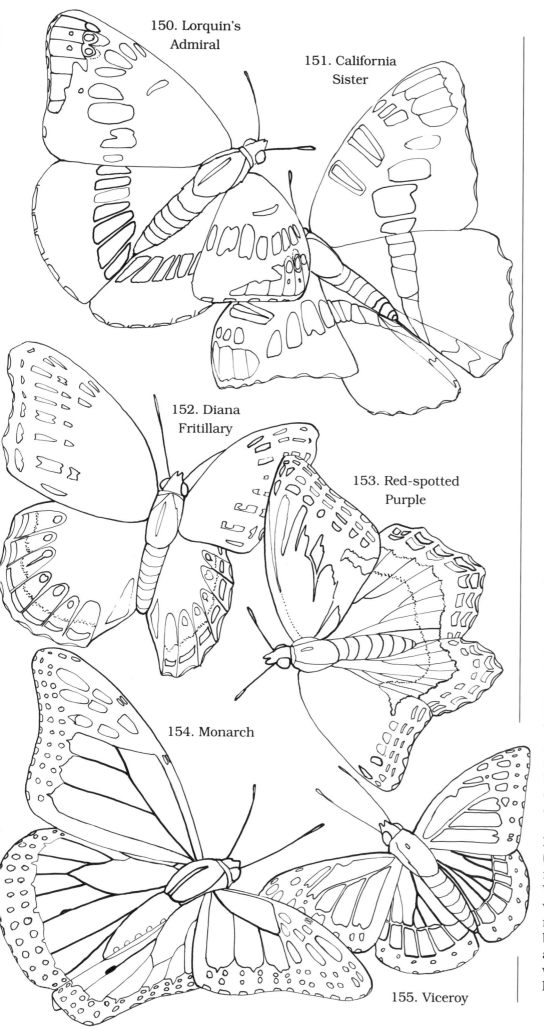

150. Lorquin's Admiral

151. California Sister

152. Diana Fritillary

153. Red-spotted Purple

154. Monarch

155. Viceroy

## Brush-footed Models and Mimics

*Many of our larger and more colorful butterflies belong to the brush-footed family, members of which have only four walking legs. Of those, a number take part in mimicry: the art of looking like one another in order to hoodwink predators like birds. Usually there is a toxic model and a tasty mimic, or else both taste bad to double-team the birds.*

**Lorquin's Admiral (150) and California Sister (151)** Butterfly watchers can tell these West Coast butterflies apart by their minor differences, but to birds they look much the same with their white stripes, black wings, and orange wing-tips. The sister feeds on oaks and chinkapins as larvae, the admiral on willows and hardhack. They have different flight patterns but are equally handsome on the wing. They probably both taste bitter to birds.

**Diana Fritillary (152) and Red-spotted Purple (153)** These are two of several butterflies that have evolved as mimics of the Pipevine Swallowtail (page 39), a poisonous insect. Once a bird gets a bite of a Pipevine, it will leave all these others alone. The purple is closely related to the Lorquin's Admiral and the Viceroy. Only the female of the Diana mimics the Pipevine; she is black with blue on her hindwings, while her mate is orange and black. The purple eats willows, the Diana violets.

**Monarch (154)** and **Viceroy (155)** The most famous mimicry partners are the Viceroy and Monarch. But while we used to think that the mimic Viceroys tasted fine to birds while the model Monarchs were toxic from the milkweed their larvae eat, we now know that both the Viceroy and the Monarch are distasteful. Monarchs are also famous for their incredible autumn migrations, when they fly south in large numbers to spend the winter in the Mexican mountains or on the California coast.

**Buckeye (156)** Sometimes great numbers of buckeyes fly south along the Atlantic coast in the autumn, and they can show up in far-flung locations. Their big, blue eyespots give them their name. They love to nectar on asters and lay their eggs on plantain.

**American Painted Lady (157)** Common and well known at butterfly gardens in the East, it is rare in the West. The related Cosmopolitan Painted Lady, famous for huge migrations, lacks this species' intense pink underside and has several small blue eyespots instead of two big ones. Look for ladies around pearly everlasting and thistles.

**Red Admiral (158)** Few sights in nature are as striking as a Red Admiral expanding its scarlet-banded black wings against the bark of a birch or an aspen tree. An old-fashioned name for this butterfly was "Red Admirable," but later someone thought the stripes looked like an admiral's shoulder epaulettes. Unlike the true admirals, whose larvae live on willows, these feed on stinging nettles.

**Mourning Cloak (159)** A very popular butterfly is the Mourning Cloak, named for the ashy black underside. Above, it is rich chocolate with blue spots and yellow rims. Cince it hibernates as an adult butterfly, it can be seen flying on a sunny day in midwinter, perhaps giving rise to its old name, the "Grand Surprise."

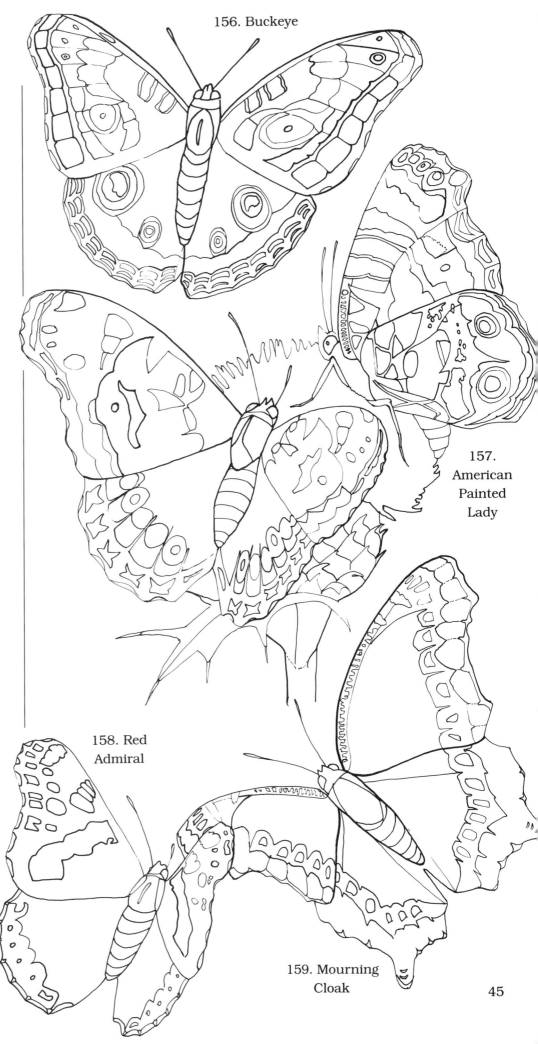

156. Buckeye

157. American Painted Lady

158. Red Admiral

159. Mourning Cloak

45

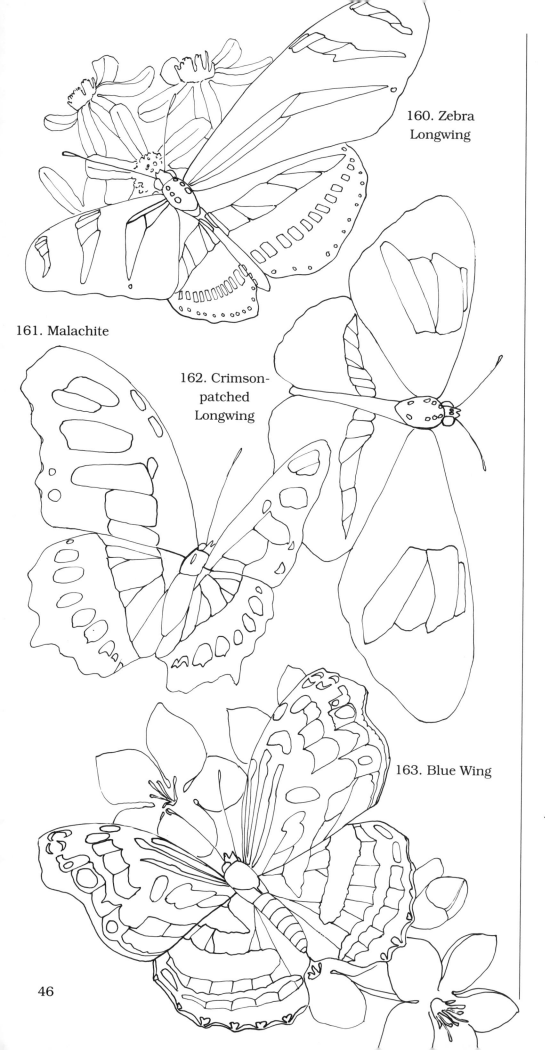

160. Zebra Longwing

161. Malachite

162. Crimson-patched Longwing

163. Blue Wing

**Zebra Longwing (160)** While the Zebra Swallowtail has black stripes on white, the Zebra Longwing has pale yellow on black. It lives only in the American tropics, including parts of Florida and Texas. It has the unique habit of roosting overnight in clusters, in wooded habitats such as the Everglades hammocks.

**Malachite (161)** Several of our most colorful butterflies just dip into the U.S. along the southern edges, where it is warm enough for their tropical habits. One of these is the jade-marbled Malachite, named for the beautiful mineral of the same color.

**Crimson-patched Longwing (162)** The longwings are a tropical American family with many mimics. They are the only butterflies known to eat pollen as well as nectar, and this is one of the few longwing species that occurs as far north as Texas. Longwing larvae feed only on passionflower vines.

**Blue Wing (163)** Another tropical visitor to our southernmost borders is the Blue Wing. Butterfly watchers in southern Texas might also see Green Wings, and in Florida, occasional Purple Wings. All of these bright, hothouse butterflies are rather rare. The deeper you go into the American tropics, the more individuals and species of butterflies you find, so there are naturally many of bright colors; but the jungles have their drab butterflies too.

# Insects of the Grasslands

Since butterflies like open, sunny, flowery places, prairies and other grasslands tend to be good habitats for them. Skippers and satyrs in particular belong to the grasslands, since their larvae feed on species of grasses and sedges. The **Regal Fritillary (164),** like other silverspots, requires violets; it is the largest American fritillary and is limited to native prairies. **Common Wood Nymphs (165),** also called Blue-eyed Graylings, flit between the grass blades, flashing their big eyespots that deflect bird attack away from their bodies. They, and **Prairie Ringlets (166),** are examples of a group of brush-foots known as the browns or satyrs, whose larvae eat grass — look for the wood nymph caterpillar on a grass blade. The **Spittlebug,** or **Froghopper (167),** is a grass-sucking true bug that makes a protective coating of spitlike fluid around itself. Silvery chevrons brand the underside of the hindwings of the **Common Branded Skipper (168),** which has a scattered range across much of the northern half of the world. The larvae of many skippers form loose cocoons in which they pupate among the grass roots.

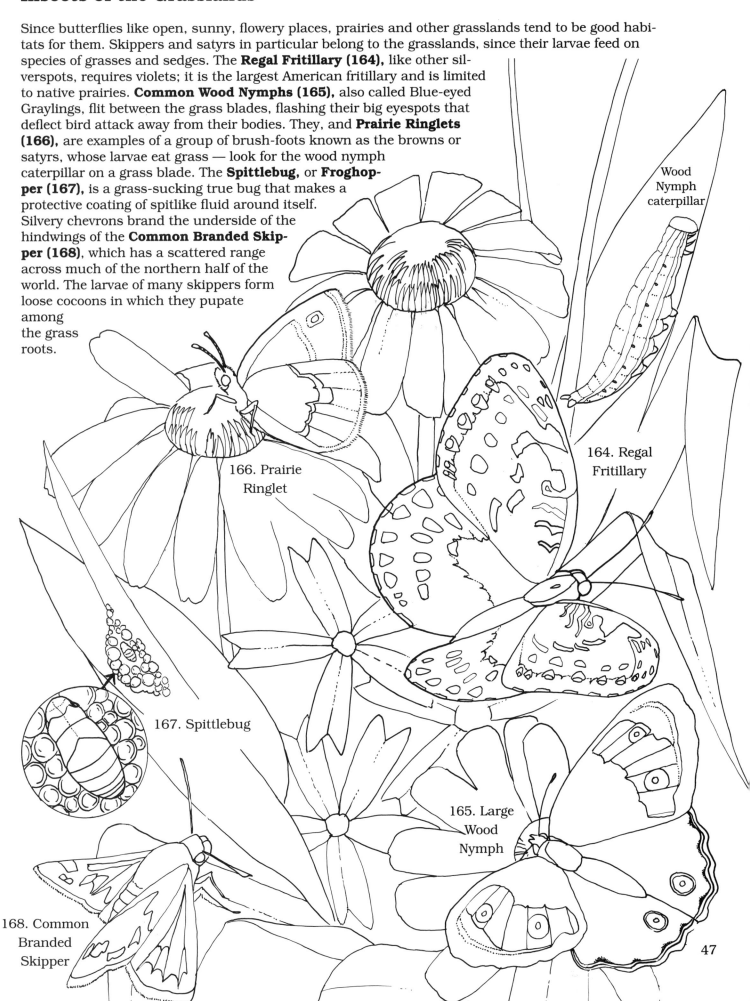

Wood Nymph caterpillar

166. Prairie Ringlet

164. Regal Fritillary

167. Spittlebug

165. Large Wood Nymph

168. Common Branded Skipper

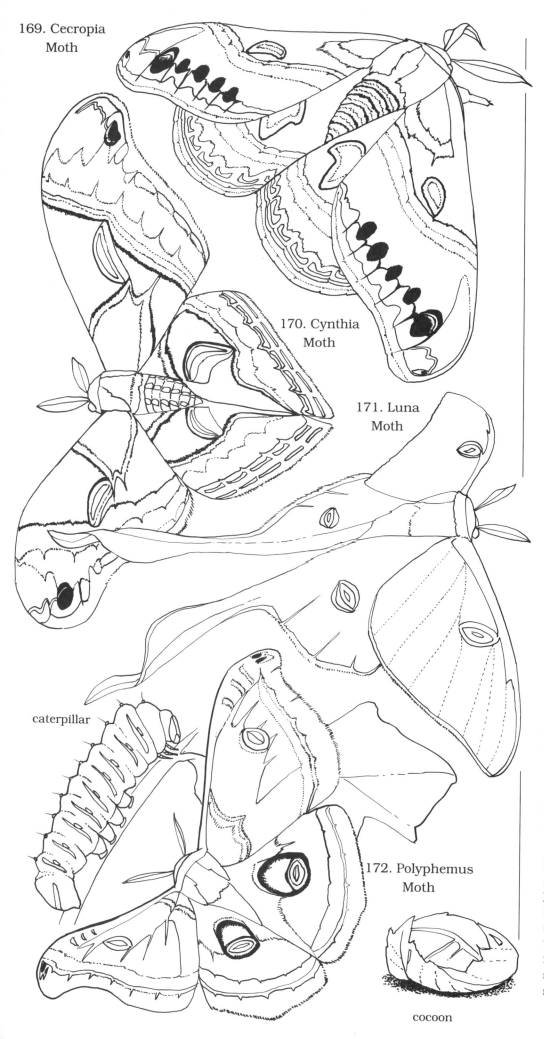

169. Cecropia Moth

170. Cynthia Moth

171. Luna Moth

caterpillar

172. Polyphemus Moth

cocoon

**Cecropia Moth (169)** Because of its rusty red, furry scales, this giant silk moth is also known as the Robin Moth. Cecropia is a bush, one of its favorite host plants; but it will feed on other trees and shrubs as well, such as lilacs, cherries, birches, and currants. It pupates in a big silken cocoon that hangs from a twig of the food plant. Adult giant silk moths do not feed at all, so their lives depend upon the fat stored by the caterpillars. The bright lights of cities interrupt the Cecropia's mating activity and make it prey to bats.

**Cynthia Moth (170)** A native of China, the Cynthia was introduced to this country in the 1800s as a possible silk source. The difficulty of unwinding the cocoon's strands ended the experiment, but the moth remained. Its big larvae feed on ailanthus, a weedy tree that grows in waste areas, so the moth is often found in old industrial parts of eastern cities. Its soft honey and lilac colors contrast with the concrete of its habitat.

**Luna Moth (171)** When people think of moths, they do not usually picture the beautiful giant silk moths. Yet throughout much of the forested East, several species of these saturniine silk moths might come to your windows or porch light. The pale green Luna Moth, with its silky white thorax and purple leading edge, is among the loveliest expressions of nature. It has a little horn on its thorax to cut its way out of the cocoon.

**Polyphemus Moth (172)** This great tan species with blue, yellow, and transparent eyespots, also found in the forest scene (page 55), lives in deciduous woodlands throughout much of North America. All stages of its life history are shown here.

**Imperial Moth (173)** Several American moths have the beautiful color scheme of yellow and royal purple, but none of the others is nearly this big. The males are more clouded with purple than the yellower females. The larvae live high up in the oaks, ashes, lindens, birches, pines, cedars, and other trees on which they feed.

**Rosy Maple Moth (174)** This is one of the smaller silk moths, and a pretty one at that, with its pink bands on narrow yellow wings. Since it feeds heavily on maples, foresters call it the Green-striped Mapleworm after its caterpillar.

**Royal Walnut Moth (175)** Also known as the Regal Moth for its grand stature and rich colors, this silk moth lives only in the East, like the other species on this page, and it is not common except in parts of the South. Its magnificent and intimidating caterpillar (also pictured here) gives the species its third name, the Hickory Horned Devil. Besides hickories, this eye-catching beast eats persimmon, sycamore, walnut, and other trees. Since it pupates underground, you might see it traveling across a lawn or street to reach a good spot to spin up. After the adult emerges the following spring, it might come to a light near your house, and you'll see why it is called "royal."

**Io Moth (176)** The sexes of this species are very different: the forewings of the females are brown and those of the males are yellow. The blue-centered bull's-eye on the hindwing is distinctive in both sexes. The caterpillars, found on corn, clover, willow, and many other plants, bear spines that can sting like a nettle — so watch, but don't touch!

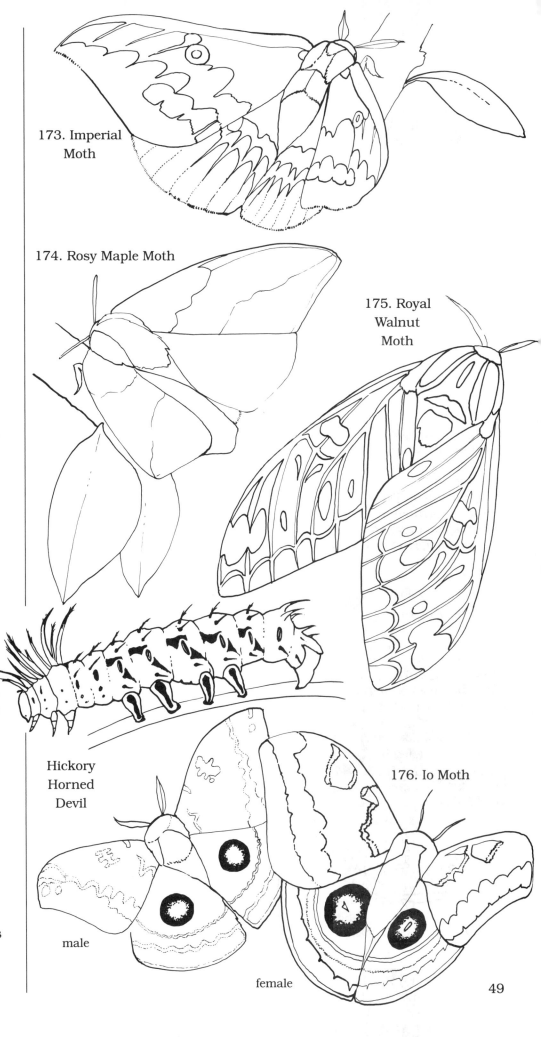

173. Imperial Moth

174. Rosy Maple Moth

175. Royal Walnut Moth

176. Io Moth

Hickory Horned Devil

male

female

49

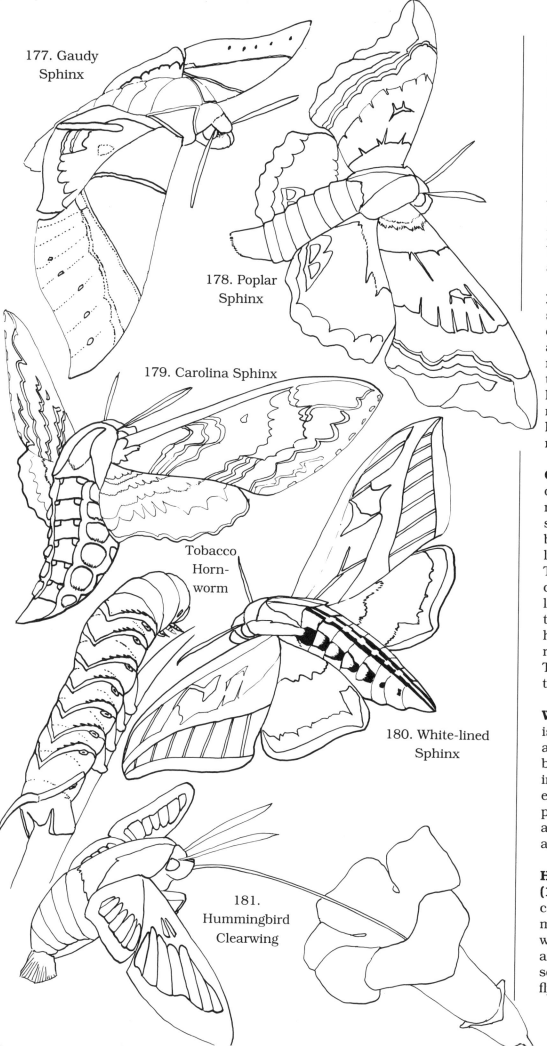

177. Gaudy Sphinx

178. Poplar Sphinx

179. Carolina Sphinx

Tobacco Hornworm

180. White-lined Sphinx

181. Hummingbird Clearwing

**Gaudy Sphinx (177)** Sphinx moths are called that because their horned caterpillars assume a sphinxlike posture when threatened. They are also called hawk moths for their narrow wings and rapid flight, and hummingbird moths, since they hover over the petunias at dusk drawing nectar with their long tongues. This southeastern hawk is particularly colorful, with its green body and forewings and yellow and red and blue hindwings.

**Poplar Sphinx (178)** This big sphinx has scalloped forewings of two-tone brown, and rosy and blue hindwings. As the name suggests, its larva has a taste for poplar, as well as willow. Before pupating, it burrows into the soil. The pupa lies naked in its chamber, with no silken cocoon around it.

**Carolina Sphinx (179)** Most common in the South but ranging widely, this large gray sphinx with its bright yellow body spots often shows up at lights. It is also known as the Tobacco Hornworm because it consumes tobacco plants and, less helpfully, potatoes and tomatoes. The caterpillar's horn is harmless. A closely related species called the Tomato Hornworm occurs farther north and west.

**White-lined Sphinx (180)** This is one of the most familiar and attractive sphinxes, flying both by day and at dusk. Not native in the North, it migrates there each year. You can attract it by planting four o'clocks. Early arrivals come to April lilacs after evening rains.

**Hummingbird Clearwing (181)** These small hawk moths can be mistaken both for hummingbirds and bumblebees, with their transparent wings and the bee-striped bodies some types have. They usually fly during the day.

**Ranchman's Tiger Moth (182)** Tiger moths tend to be spotted and striped with colorful reds and oranges and to have fuzzy larvae. This large one is common on western ranchlands and has similar eastern relatives. Moths are often specific about which plants the caterpillars eat, but tigers are not too picky, feeding on many sorts of plants.

**Garden Tiger Moth (183)** Also known as the Great Tiger, it lives around the world in the North, but it is more common in Europe than here. The deep brown furry scales on the thorax look a little like the head of a long-eared cocker spaniel. Tiger moths are the family Arctiidae, and this one is in the group named *Arctia*, because they often live in arctic and high mountain places.

**Colona Moth (184)** This big, bright tiger occupies the southeastern coastal plain — it is not arctic. Its hindwings are clear pale yellow except for one small black spot.

**Isabella Moth (185)** Many people love this moth without knowing it, for its larva is the famous Woolly Bear. The furry caterpillar, rusty red in the middle and black on both ends, wanders the roads and fields in search of a good place to hibernate in the fall. The next spring it resumes feeding, then pupates and becomes the pale orange moth known as Isabella. The width of the caterpillar's red band varies with age, not with the severity of winter.

**Cinnabar Moth (186)** Because this moth is gorgeous and flies by day, people think it is a butterfly. Not a native of the U.S., it was imported to fight tansy ragweed, which it does very well. Kids know the stripy larvae as Tansy Tigers.

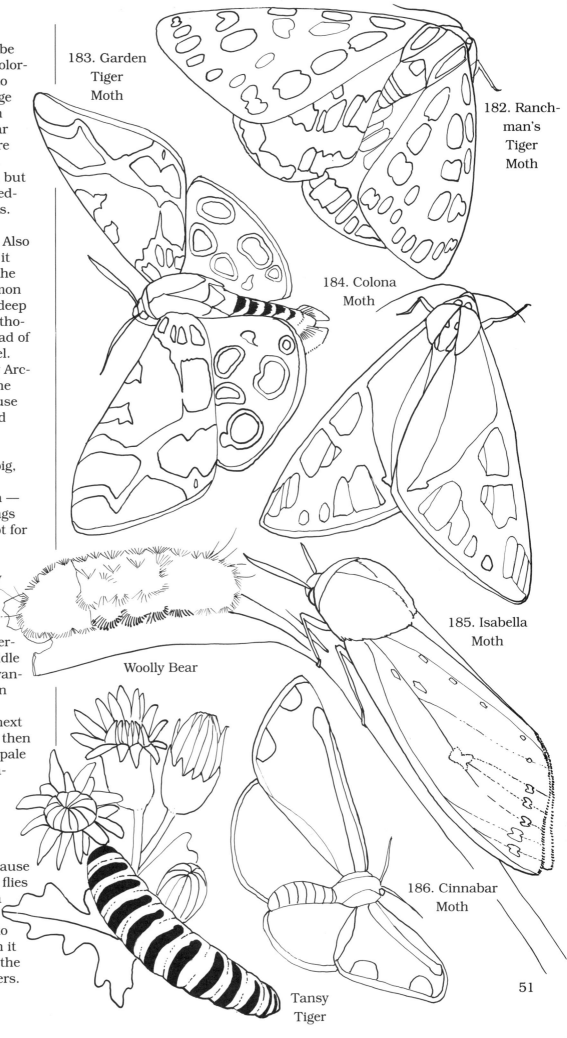

183. Garden Tiger Moth

182. Ranchman's Tiger Moth

184. Colona Moth

185. Isabella Moth

Woolly Bear

186. Cinnabar Moth

Tansy Tiger

51

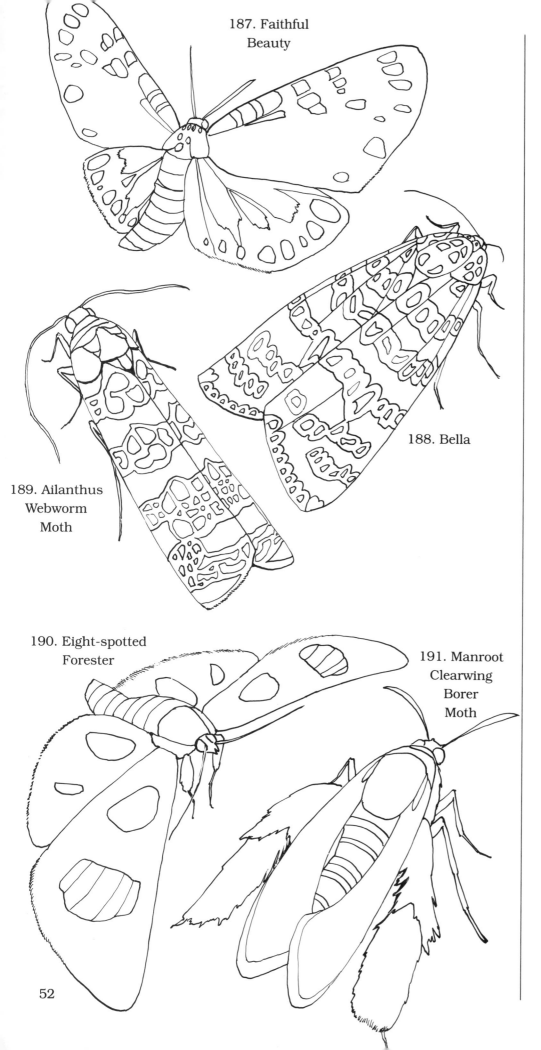

187. Faithful
Beauty

189. Ailanthus
Webworm
Moth

188. Bella

190. Eight-spotted
Forester

191. Manroot
Clearwing
Borer
Moth

**Faithful Beauty (187)** One of the fairest of American moths, it flies by day, year-round, among the Florida hardwood hammocks. It is clearly a beauty, but "faithful" only by virtue of its Latin name *(fidelissima)*. Because its caterpillars consume toxic plants like oleander and devil's potato, it tastes bad, and its bright colors warn birds to leave it alone.

**Bella (188)** "Bella" means beauty, and this common little eastern species surely is one. Its pink and orange colors make an almost shocking combination. Like the Faithful Beauty (and unlike most moths, which fly by night), Bella flies in the daytime and warns off birds with its bright colors.

**Ailanthus Webworm Moth (189)** Like the Cynthia Moth, this species' caterpillars feed on ailanthus, or tree-of-heaven, where they make communal nests. This is one of the so-called micro-moths — yet it can reach an inch or more in wingspan, while some "micros" spread no wider than the dash in this sentence.

**Eight-spotted Forester (190)** Commonly, even in cities in the Midwest, one sees these orange-legged, spotty day-fliers nectaring at sweet rocket and other flowers. They lay their eggs on grapes and Virginia creeper, the preferred caterpillar food plants.

**Manroot Clearwing Borer Moth (191)** With its furry, reddish hindlegs and yellow-striped body, this looks like the fiercest wasp you ever saw; but its antennae and gray wings give it away as a harmless moth. Its caterpillars bore into huge wild cucumbers.

**Sweetheart Underwing (192)**
Several moths on this page are members of the huge Noctuidae family. They include the familiar "millers" (named for their powdery appearance, as if they were dusted with flour), of which this species is a fancy type. Many underwing species dwell in eastern deciduous forests, fewer in the West. Its scientific name, *amatrix,* means sweetheart, reflecting the whimsical and romantic nature of early lepidopterists. The Sweetheart's hindwings are banded in beautiful pinks, reds, yellows, and oranges.

**Locust Underwing (193)** Not closely related to the Sweetheart and her cousins, this type of underwing feeds on locust trees. When underwing moths lie at rest on bark or stone, their camouflaged forewings close, making them nearly invisible. If a bird then comes near, they flash their bright hindwings (or "underwings"), startling the intruder long enough to escape.

**Hieroglyphic Moth (194)** This spectacular moth looks nothing like its relatives, the dingy millers. The family name, Noctuidae, means "denizen of the night" and could apply to most moths. Its caterpillars feed on plants from pecans to sweet potatoes around the Gulf Coast, and the adults sometimes stray into the North.

**Great Leopard Moth (195)**
Several members of the Prominent family of moths, including the Tentacled Prominent and the Great Leopard Moth, have boldly marked adults and outrageous caterpillars. In its threat posture, the larva's head hunches up and fierce red horns poke out of its tail. After feeding on willows, the larva forms a hard cocoon of silk and bits of bark and cements it to a branch or fence post.

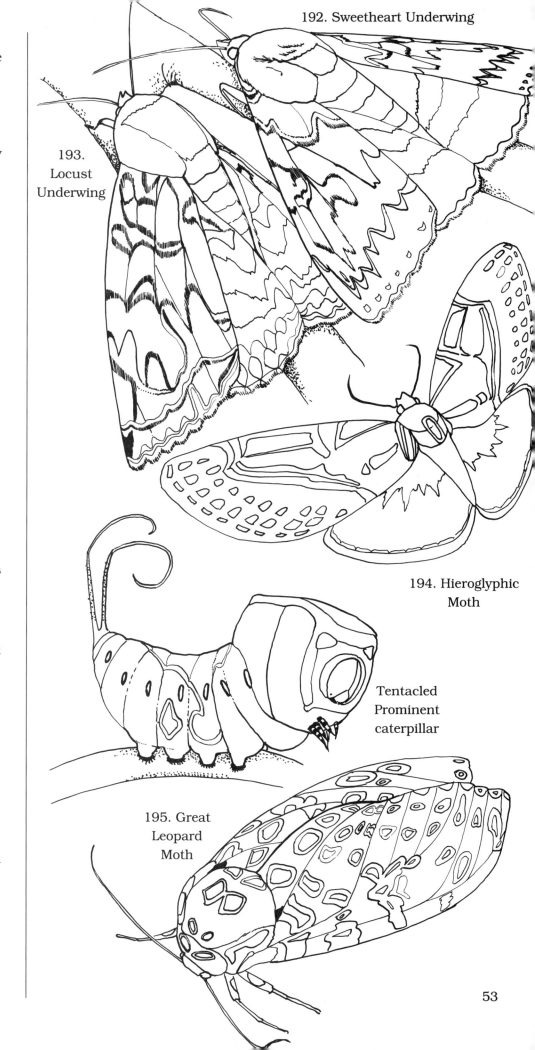

192. Sweetheart Underwing

193. Locust Underwing

194. Hieroglyphic Moth

Tentacled Prominent caterpillar

195. Great Leopard Moth

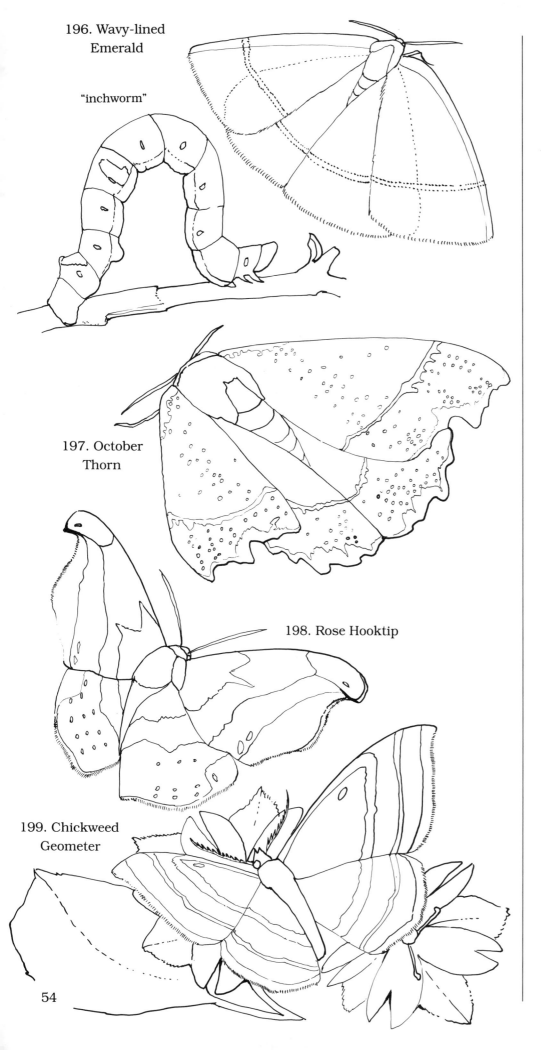

196. Wavy-lined Emerald

"inchworm"

197. October Thorn

198. Rose Hooktip

199. Chickweed Geometer

**Wavy-lined Emerald (196)** Another large family is that of the geometer (meaning "measuring the earth") or inchworm moths. They tend to hold their wings like butterflies, and many fly by day, but they have the feathery or threadlike antennae of moths and a weak, fluttery flight. Several related groups of these green emeralds occur in all parts of the country, feeding on many kinds of plants and often coming to lights. Some people mistake it for a little Luna Moth, a more famous green moth.

**October Thorn (Maple Spanworm) (197)** Moths often have two names, one for the adults and one for the hungry caterpillars. Of course, the larvae are not "worms" at all. Some consider this handsome big geometer a forest pest on hardwoods. But others value its annual appearance at the porch lights in October, when most of the other moths and butterflies are gone.

**Rose Hooktip (198)** Hooktips are a small, distinct family related to the geometers and resembling them. They have two peculiar characteristics: their forewings end in a hook, and their larvae lack any rear legs so the back end sticks up. You might spot these unusual caterpillars on viburnums or birches. The amount of rosy purple on this species varies from none to lots, with many individuals mottled like a tiny Imperial Moth.

**Chickweed Geometer (199)** This pretty little inchworm moth is familiar to children because it is at home in lawns and vacant lots. Feeding on chickweeds, knotweeds, clovers, and other common plants as a larva, it is both widespread and numerous over the eastern half of North America.

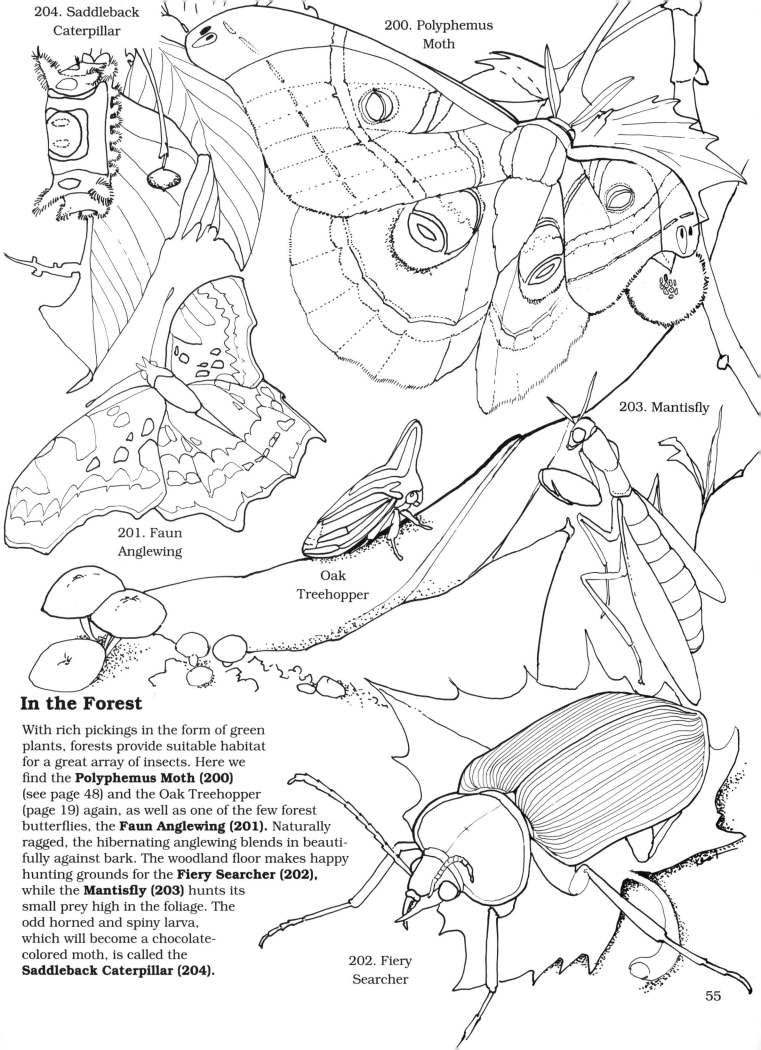

**204. Saddleback Caterpillar**

**200. Polyphemus Moth**

**203. Mantisfly**

**201. Faun Anglewing**

Oak Treehopper

## In the Forest

With rich pickings in the form of green plants, forests provide suitable habitat for a great array of insects. Here we find the **Polyphemus Moth (200)** (see page 48) and the Oak Treehopper (page 19) again, as well as one of the few forest butterflies, the **Faun Anglewing (201).** Naturally ragged, the hibernating anglewing blends in beautifully against bark. The woodland floor makes happy hunting grounds for the **Fiery Searcher (202),** while the **Mantisfly (203)** hunts its small prey high in the foliage. The odd horned and spiny larva, which will become a chocolate-colored moth, is called the **Saddleback Caterpillar (204).**

**202. Fiery Searcher**

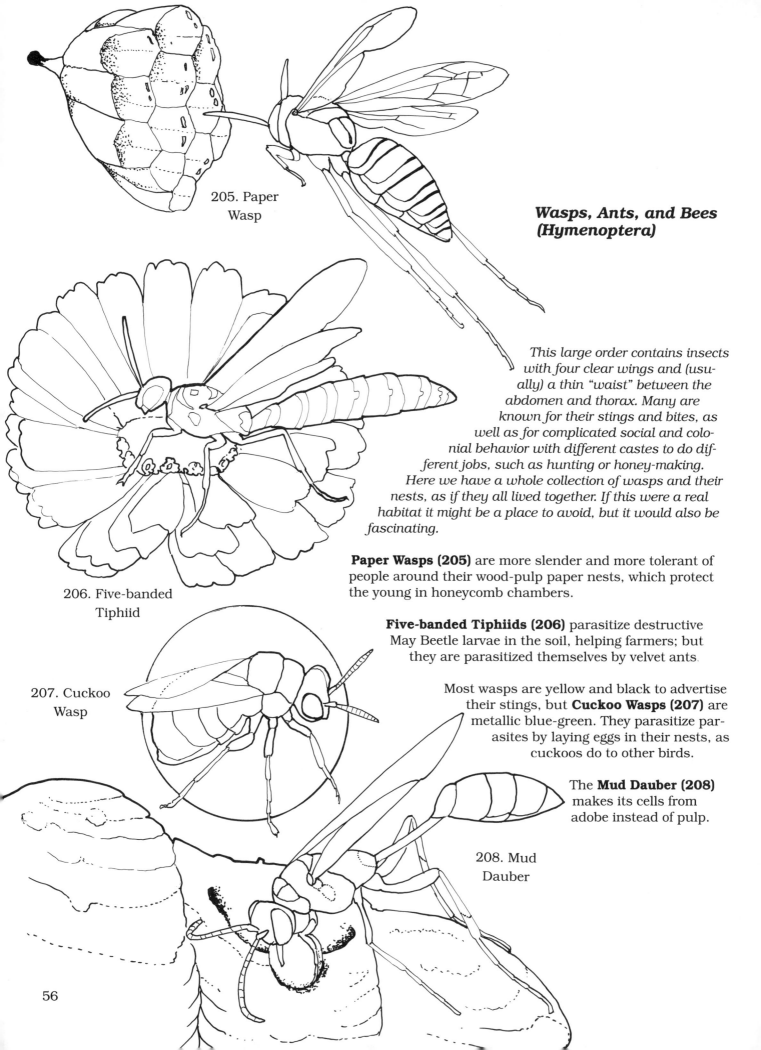

205. Paper Wasp

## Wasps, Ants, and Bees (Hymenoptera)

206. Five-banded Tiphiid

207. Cuckoo Wasp

208. Mud Dauber

*This large order contains insects with four clear wings and (usually) a thin "waist" between the abdomen and thorax. Many are known for their stings and bites, as well as for complicated social and colonial behavior with different castes to do different jobs, such as hunting or honey-making. Here we have a whole collection of wasps and their nests, as if they all lived together. If this were a real habitat it might be a place to avoid, but it would also be fascinating.*

**Paper Wasps (205)** are more slender and more tolerant of people around their wood-pulp paper nests, which protect the young in honeycomb chambers.

**Five-banded Tiphiids (206)** parasitize destructive May Beetle larvae in the soil, helping farmers; but they are parasitized themselves by velvet ants.

Most wasps are yellow and black to advertise their stings, but **Cuckoo Wasps (207)** are metallic blue-green. They parasitize parasites by laying eggs in their nests, as cuckoos do to other birds.

The **Mud Dauber (208)** makes its cells from adobe instead of pulp.

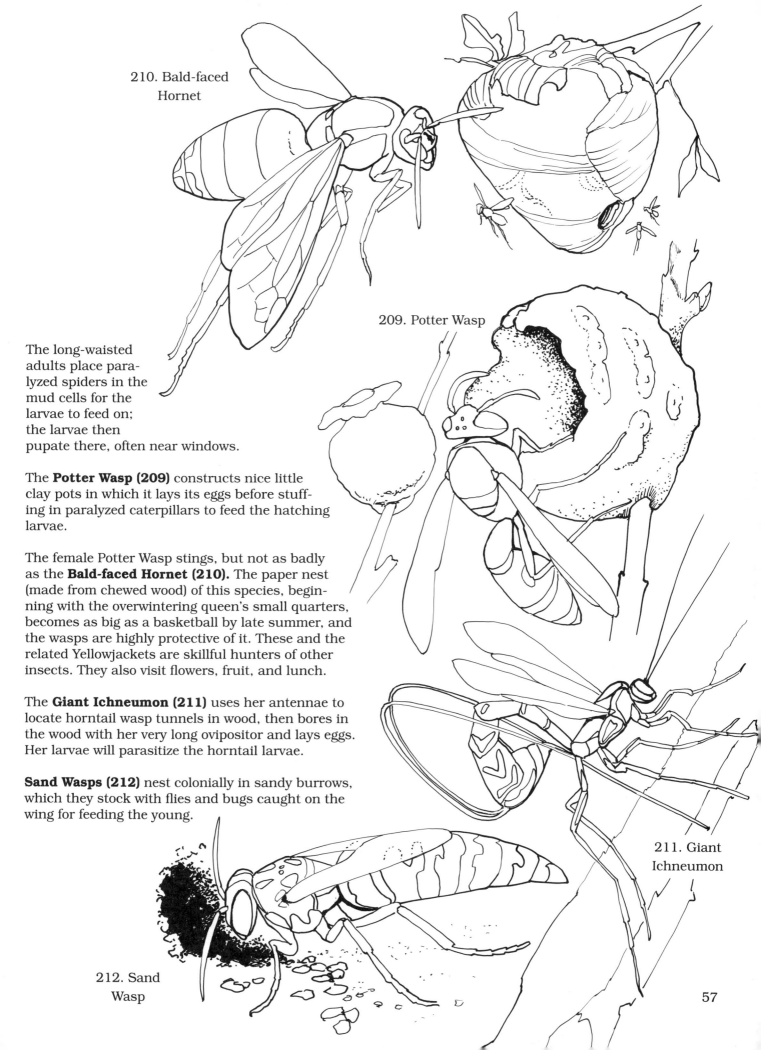

210. Bald-faced
Hornet

209. Potter Wasp

The long-waisted
adults place para-
lyzed spiders in the
mud cells for the
larvae to feed on;
the larvae then
pupate there, often near windows.

The **Potter Wasp (209)** constructs nice little
clay pots in which it lays its eggs before stuff-
ing in paralyzed caterpillars to feed the hatching
larvae.

The female Potter Wasp stings, but not as badly
as the **Bald-faced Hornet (210)**. The paper nest
(made from chewed wood) of this species, beginning with the overwintering queen's small quarters,
becomes as big as a basketball by late summer, and
the wasps are highly protective of it. These and the
related Yellowjackets are skillful hunters of other
insects. They also visit flowers, fruit, and lunch.

The **Giant Ichneumon (211)** uses her antennae to
locate horntail wasp tunnels in wood, then bores in
the wood with her very long ovipositor and lays eggs.
Her larvae will parasitize the horntail larvae.

**Sand Wasps (212)** nest colonially in sandy burrows,
which they stock with flies and bugs caught on the
wing for feeding the young.

211. Giant
Ichneumon

212. Sand
Wasp

57

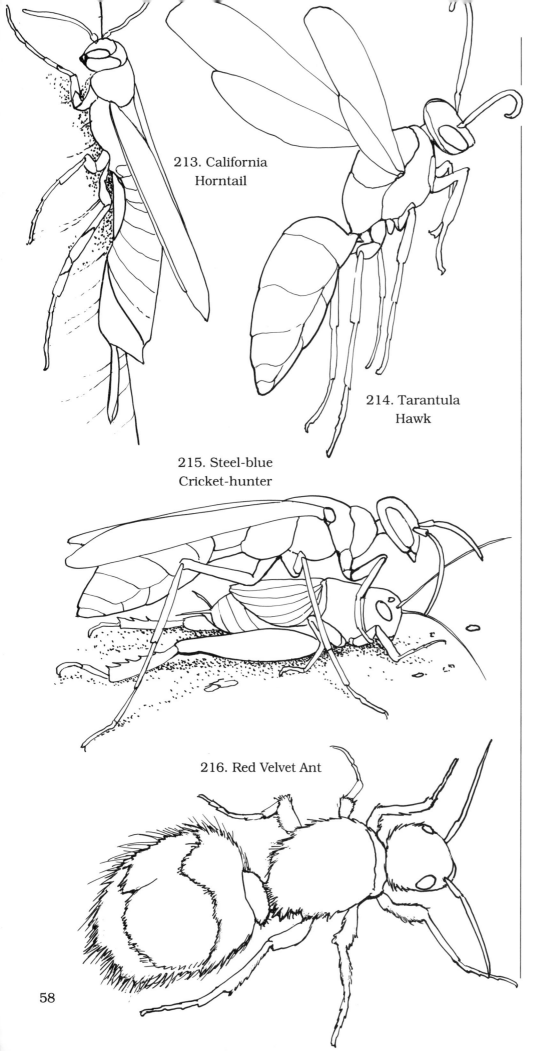

213. California Horntail

214. Tarantula Hawk

215. Steel-blue Cricket-hunter

216. Red Velvet Ant

**California Horntail (213)** Big, stout, and cylindrical, horntails look scary, but they do not sting. The impressive "horn" on the "tail" serves as a drill for laying eggs under the bark of trees. There the larvae feed, emerging later through a large hole. The adults feed on flower nectar and visit water. Don't expect to see horntails commonly.

**Tarantula Hawk (214)** Many wasps prey on spiders. This and related species attack the biggest spiders, tarantulas and trapdoor spiders. After paralyzing the prey with a powerful sting, the wasp lays an egg in its body. The wasp larva will eat its way out of the still-living spider. You can recognize these dry-country wasps by their big red wings and blue-black bodies.

**Steel-blue Cricket-hunter (215)** Sometimes you'll see these shiny wasps digging burrows in sandy paths or roadsides. Then they catch and sting a grasshopper or cricket, drag it into the hole, and leave an egg behind. A similar blue-black wasp invades the nests of Mud Daubers, stealing their spiders. And still other hunting wasps stalk sphinx moth caterpillars.

**Red Velvet Ant (216)** Although they look and act like ants, and the females are wingless, these desert dwellers are actually wasps. Other species live in sandy spots across the continent. They invade the brood nests of bumblebees in the larval form, eating the bee brood. Adults visit flowers for nectar. Because their colorful "fur" makes them so attractive, people are tempted to handle velvet ants. Don't do it! Their sting is so strong that this species has been given another name: "cow killer."

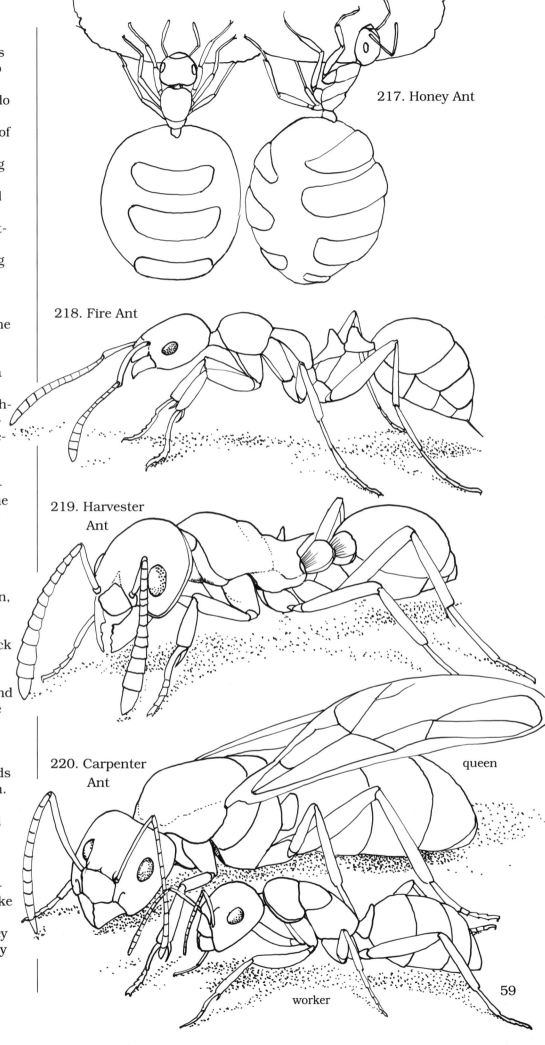

**Honey Ant (217)** One of the most interesting traits of ants is the way labor is divided up through the use of castes, or social classes specialized to do certain jobs. An extreme example is the storage caste of Honey Ants. Workers gather nectar from flowers and bring it back to the storage ants, who hang with their enlarged abdomens full of honey for when it is needed. Southwestern Indians sought out the colonies to gather these living honey pots.

217. Honey Ant

**Fire Ant (218)** These ants build their nest mounds in the ground. Workers have no wings as the reproductive adults do, but they possess a powerful sting that gives the species its name. In the southern states, Fire Ants are considered a nuisance and sometimes a threat to safety. But some entomologists believe they are beneficial in controlling other insects and that the chemicals used to fight them have done more harm than the ants themselves.

218. Fire Ant

**Harvester Ant (219)** Ants have a big head and abdomen, a narrower thorax, and a humped "waist" or pedicel in between. This type has a black head and red abdomen, but there are variations on that theme. They harvest seeds and other organic material. There are several Harvester Ant species across the country. Relatives like the Western Thatch Ant may build mounds of debris four or five feet high.

219. Harvester Ant

**Carpenter Ant (220)** Several species of Carpenter Ants occur across North America. They are so-called because they excavate galleries in rotting wood in which to live. Like termites, they can damage houses, but unlike them, they cannot eat wood. Instead they like fruit and other sweet things as well as insects.

220. Carpenter Ant

queen

worker

59

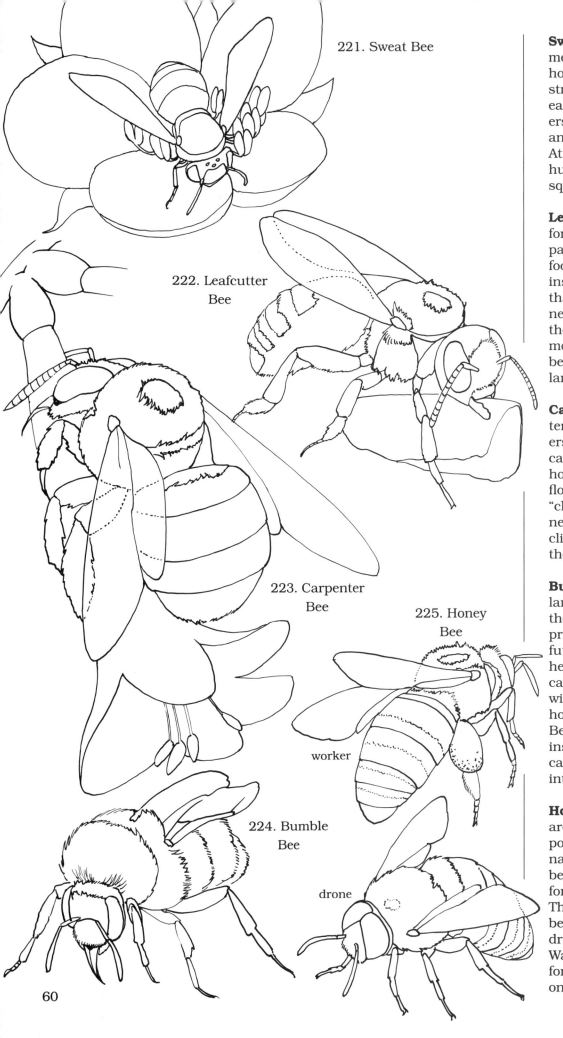

221. Sweat Bee

222. Leafcutter
Bee

223. Carpenter
Bee

225. Honey
Bee

worker

224. Bumble
Bee

drone

**Sweat Bee (221)** These bright metallic green bees nest in holes they dig in dirt cliffs, dry streambanks — any vertical earth surface. They visit flowers for nectar and pollen to eat and take home for their young. Attracted to perspiring humans, they sting only if squeezed, and then weakly.

**Leafcutter Bee (222)** To care for their young, these bees prepare a nursery complete with food. Having dug a hole, they insert bits of leaf and petal that they have cut, along with nectar, pollen, and an egg; then they seal the hole with more leaf fragments. These bees are often placed in croplands to help with pollination.

**Carpenter Bee (223)** Carpenter Bees can alarm homeowners, but they seldom sting or cause significant damage to houses. Carpenter Bees visit flowers, and some types "cheat" by nipping into the nectar chamber instead of climbing inside and pollinating the plant.

**Bumble Bee (224)** In these largest of American bees, only the queen overwinters. She produces workers, drones, and future queens in the spring. In her nest, a vole hole or other cavity, she feeds the larvae with pollen and herself from a honeypot of nectar. Bumble Bees are delightful, helpful insects, but they sting, so be careful to watch them without interfering in their business.

**Honey Bee (225)** Some people are allergic to the sting of this popular insect. It is not a native. Settlers brought these bees from Europe in the 1600s for the honey they produce. They have a complex social behavior with castes (male drone and worker are shown). Watch for wild bee-trees, and for bright yellow pollen baskets on bees' hindlegs.

# In the Mountains

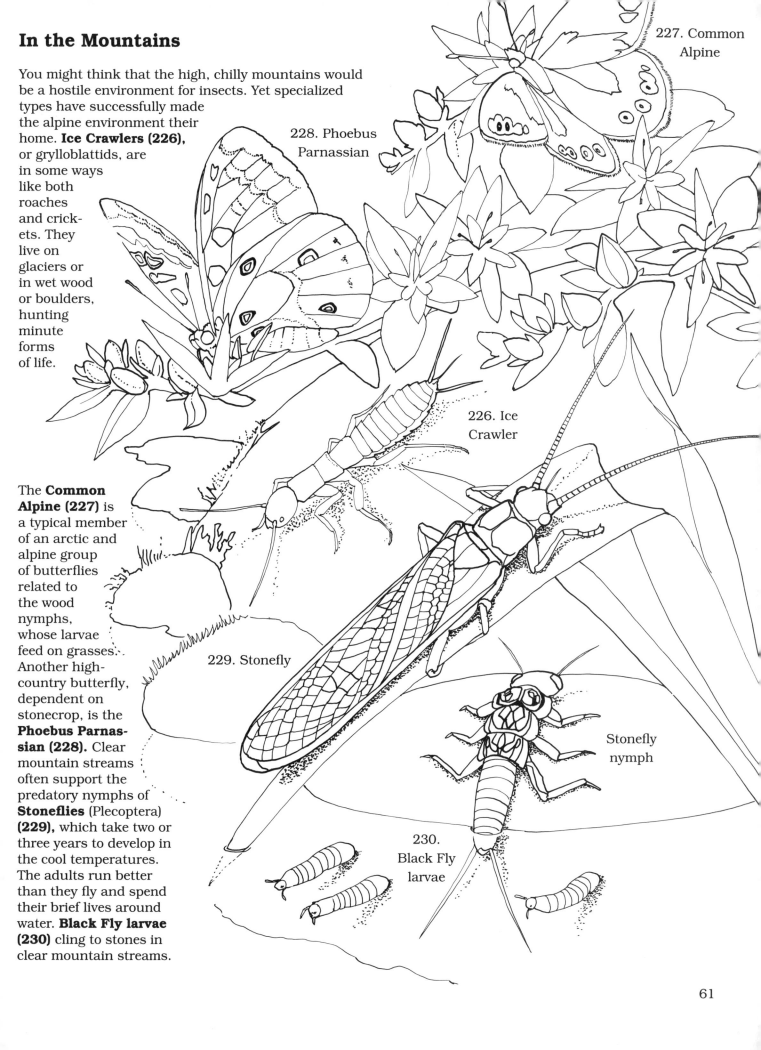

You might think that the high, chilly mountains would be a hostile environment for insects. Yet specialized types have successfully made the alpine environment their home. **Ice Crawlers (226),** or grylloblattids, are in some ways like both roaches and crickets. They live on glaciers or in wet wood or boulders, hunting minute forms of life.

The **Common Alpine (227)** is a typical member of an arctic and alpine group of butterflies related to the wood nymphs, whose larvae feed on grasses. Another high-country butterfly, dependent on stonecrop, is the **Phoebus Parnassian (228).** Clear mountain streams often support the predatory nymphs of **Stoneflies** (Plecoptera) **(229),** which take two or three years to develop in the cool temperatures. The adults run better than they fly and spend their brief lives around water. **Black Fly larvae (230)** cling to stones in clear mountain streams.

227. Common Alpine

228. Phoebus Parnassian

226. Ice Crawler

229. Stonefly

Stonefly nymph

230. Black Fly larvae

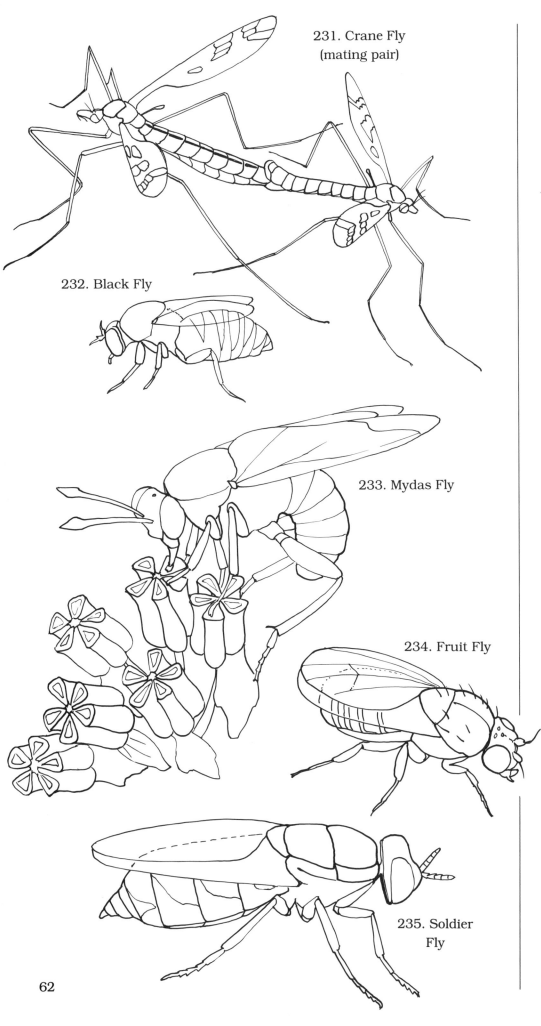

231. Crane Fly
(mating pair)

232. Black Fly

233. Mydas Fly

234. Fruit Fly

235. Soldier
Fly

## Flies (Diptera)

*The true flies have only two wings (di-ptera) and a thicker connection between abdomen and thorax than bees. They also tend to have very large compound eyes that dominate a head with a skinny neck. Both helpful and harmful species of flies are extremely numerous, diverse, and widespread. Many types mimic bees and wasps, though the flies cannot sting.*

**Crane Fly (231)** Thousands of species of crane flies live all over North America. With their very long legs dangling, they look like huge mosquitoes, but they cannot bite. They often get trapped inside windows.

**Black Fly (232)** Among the worst of biting insects, along with mosquitoes, are the dreaded black flies. They can actually weaken or kill wildlife and livestock, and some species carry human diseases, while others are just highly irritating. The larvae cling to stones in swift streams, the flies' required habitat.

**Mydas Fly (233)** Mydas flies are named for their clubbed antennae, which reminded the namer of mythical King Midas's donkey ears. Despite those butterflylike antennae and a wasplike appearance, they have only two wings, like all other flies.

**Fruit Fly (234)** Fruit flies show up wherever there is overripe fruit. Few other organisms have been as important in the study of genetics. Look for their bright red eyes.

**Soldier Fly (235)** These attractive, colorful flies range over much of the continent. They live around ponds and streams, where their larvae feed on algae while the adults visit flowers.

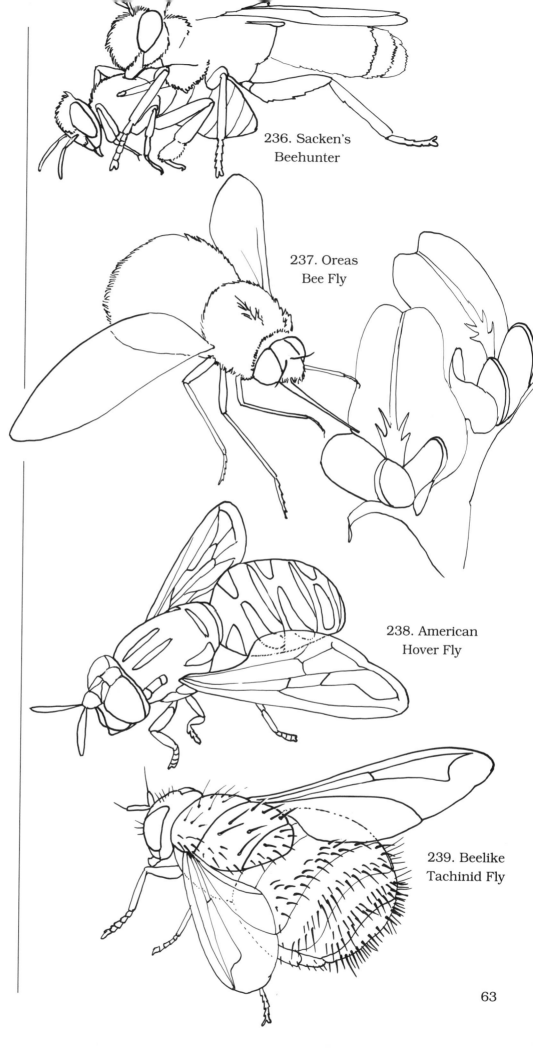

## Sacken's Beehunter (236)

This big furry fly looks a bit like a bee but is a West Coast member of the robber fly family. Efficient predators, robbers lock onto the thorax of their prey (in this case, bees) from above, giving them no chance of escape. The beehunter then pierces its prey with its proboscis and sucks out its juices.

236. Sacken's Beehunter

## Oreas Bee Fly (237)

Of the many insects that mimic stinging bees and wasps, bee flies are among the best. Their fat, furry bodies and two (not four) wings let you tell them from bees. With long tongues, or proboscies, they probe flowers for nectar. Their larvae parasitize many kinds of insects. This golden species of the West has relatives all over.

237. Oreas Bee Fly

## American Hover Fly (238)

Like bee flies, hover flies hover in place, visit flowers, and mimic stinging insects — usually wasps instead of bees. Both hover flies and bee flies are fun to watch in the field and garden and do not sting or bite. Since they need pollen for proper development of the eggs, adults of both kinds are important pollinators. The larvae of this hover fly are valuable aphid hunters. Hover flies undergo notable migrations, showing up in strange places far from their breeding grounds in the autumn.

238. American Hover Fly

## Beelike Tachinid Fly (239)

Tachinid flies are unpopular with butterfly watchers and gardeners because their maggots parasitize caterpillars. It can be disappointing to await the emergence of a butterfly from its chrysalis, only to have a big fly come out instead; or to see a tachinid maggot eat its way out of your caterpillar. But these big, red, bristly flies are interesting themselves and important in the control of damaging kinds of moths.

239. Beelike Tachinid Fly

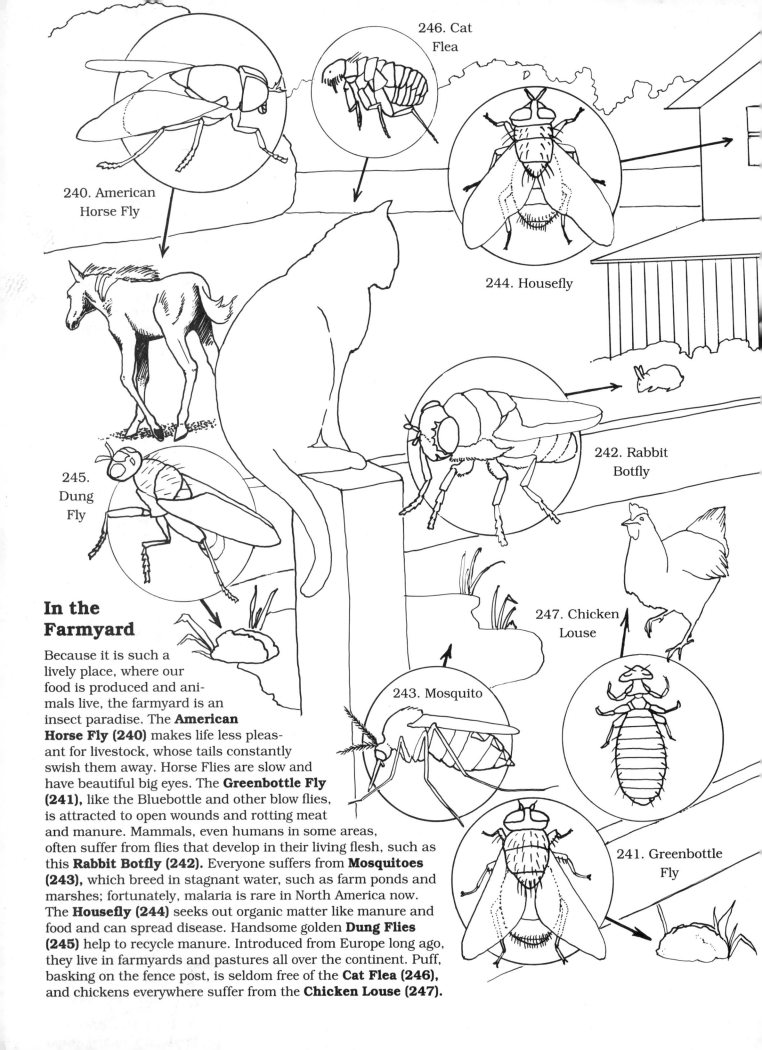

240. American Horse Fly

246. Cat Flea

244. Housefly

245. Dung Fly

242. Rabbit Botfly

247. Chicken Louse

243. Mosquito

241. Greenbottle Fly

## In the Farmyard

Because it is such a lively place, where our food is produced and animals live, the farmyard is an insect paradise. The **American Horse Fly (240)** makes life less pleasant for livestock, whose tails constantly swish them away. Horse Flies are slow and have beautiful big eyes. The **Greenbottle Fly (241),** like the Bluebottle and other blow flies, is attracted to open wounds and rotting meat and manure. Mammals, even humans in some areas, often suffer from flies that develop in their living flesh, such as this **Rabbit Botfly (242).** Everyone suffers from **Mosquitoes (243),** which breed in stagnant water, such as farm ponds and marshes; fortunately, malaria is rare in North America now. The **Housefly (244)** seeks out organic matter like manure and food and can spread disease. Handsome golden **Dung Flies (245)** help to recycle manure. Introduced from Europe long ago, they live in farmyards and pastures all over the continent. Puff, basking on the fence post, is seldom free of the **Cat Flea (246),** and chickens everywhere suffer from the **Chicken Louse (247).**